The Secret Life of Jesse James

In *The Secret Life of Jesse James*, the first epistolary western novel, Arthur Winfield Knight captures the inner life of Jesse James through a series of letters written by the 19th-century outlaw to his mother, his sister Susan, his brother Frank, his cousin and wife Zee, his friend Cole Younger and a few other people, including Belle Starr, Major John Newman Edwards and Allan Pinkerton.

The letters begin in 1864, when young Jesse is riding with Confederate legends Quantrill and Anderson during the waning days of the Civil War, and continue through his hey-day as America's most notorious and celebrated bank robber. Knight's imaginary letters provide an illuminating insight into the tragedy of the botched Northfield Raid, the births (and deaths) of Jesse's children, the outlaw's passing acquaintance with Billy the Kid and the movers and shakers of the Reconstruction Era, and his untimely gangland-style "execution" in 1882 at the hand of his friend Bob Ford.

Throughout the work, Knight adheres to the historical record of America's first and most famous existential antihero, weaving contemporary news accounts and anecdotal information into a fascinating and literary western adventure.

"I've always been fascinated by America's most famous outlaw, and Jesse James really comes to life in this beautifully written book. From the Cowboy West I send my congratulations."

Prof. Mark Harris
—*Bang the Drum Slowly*

The Secret Life of Jesse James

Arthur Winfield Knight

Burnhill Wolf

321 Prospect Street NW, Lenoir NC 28645

First Edition

ISBN 0-9645655-2-8

Published by BurnhillWolf, 321 Prospect Street NW, Lenoir, NC 28645

For Kit, my Zee

1864-1868

3

Centralia, Missouri
September 1864

Dear Ma,

I don't know what day it is. (Am I 16 or 17 now?) We can scarcely keep track of months and years there has been so much fighting.

Yesterday we killed a dozen soldiers in Goslin's Lane, capturing a wagon train of provisions, and today we must have killed 350 men.

When we spotted the Yankees, they were near the rise of a hill, about half a mile distant, They dismounted, preparing to fight, and when Frank saw them he said, "The fools are going to fight us on foot. God help them."

We dismounted to tighten the cinches on the horses, then at the word of command started our charge.

Our line was nearly a quarter mile long; theirs was a lot closer together. We were about 600 yards away, our speed increasing and our ranks closing up, when they fired their first and only time. They nearly all fired over our heads.

We were laying low on our horses, a trick we learned from the Commanches, so only two of our men were killed but they were riding on either side of me.

The blood and brains from Shepherd splashed on my pants leg as he fell from his horse and I heard the man on my other side cry out, "Jesse, I'm hit," and those were the last words he ever said. We'd fought side by side in several battles, so it hurt to leave him like that but there was no stopping.

We went up the hill yelling like Indians, shrieking, and we reached the Yankee line in what seemed like seconds. Some of them were at "fix bayonets," some were biting off their cartridges, preparing to reload, but we never gave them time. Yelling, shooting our pistols, we crested the hill.

Some of the Yanks tried to run but we rode them down, killing them. Their blood turned the corn and meadow red, and all you could smell was gunpowder. All you could hear were the screams of the wounded. The dying. Every blue

4

belly in the battle was shot through the head.

Arch Clements had the best horse so he shot the first and the last man killed, but I shot the commander of the Federal troops, Major Johnson. We were almost face to face when I fired my revolver and just before I pulled the trigger I looked up at the blue sky and said, "Major, it's a good day to die."

I don't think he believed that.

When it was all over Anderson said, "That was a job well done," but most of us just stood there, too tired, too shaken to talk.

Love,
Jesse

Ray County, Missouri
mid-October 1864

Dear Frank,

Yesterday we discovered a house of prostitution near the Union encampment. Since I'm the only person in Anderson's company who has what he calls a "baby face" (I'm the only one who doesn't shave) he ordered me to put on a dress, then I was supposed to lure any Union troops I saw into the house.

When I saw three blue bellies ride by late that afternoon, I was standing in the doorway. I smiled at them, feeling like a fool, and said, "Hey soldiers. Are you looking for a good time?"

"What do you have in mind?" one of them asked.

"Whatever it is, I don't think we can do it while the three of you are on your horses and I'm standing here."

They rode over to take a closer look at me and I tried to scrunch down into my dress, hiding my face in the bonnet I wore.

The blue belly who'd spoken before said, "How much will this good time you're talking about cost?"

I didn't know how to answer that so I thought a minute, then said, "Why don't we see how much fun we have first? Then we can talk about the price."

I could hear some of the prostitutes whispering behind me, then I thought I heard one of our boys laugh. I just hoped none of the Yankees heard it.

"I don't know," the blue belly said.

"I guarantee you'll have a time you'll never forget."

The three talked for a moment, then they dismounted. I'd already gone into the parlor.

Anderson's men were out of sight, but three of the women were there in their slips. When the blue bellies came inside, the women took the rest of their clothes off.

All they were wearing were their smiles when Anderson came into the room holding a shotgun. He yelled, "Havin' a good time, boys?"

The three Yanks were laughing, but they never laughed again.

Anderson let them have it with both barrels.

One of the Yanks had a dazed kind of a look as his body slid down the wall, painting it with his blood, and the one I'd been talking to flipped over the couch, backwards, when the blast hit him. Before the third one could get his pistol out of its holster, the place where his face had been disappeared and I heard another shotgun blast.

I don't think the whole thing lasted longer than thirty seconds.

When I threw off my dress, some of the boys started to laugh. "Hey, Jess," one of them said. "You look so good in that maybe you could get a job here."

Someone else said, "He wouldn't want to deprive your mother of work."

That's one thing I hate about war. It makes men ugly.

Sometimes I get mad at Ma for being so overbearing with us, but I'd never say a thing like that.

I went outside, standing on the porch in the late afternoon sun. I could see my breath in the air and there was a small field of pumpkins next to the house and I thought of that old rhyme: When the frost is on the pumpkin, that's the time for peter dunkin' and I could hear the laughter of the men inside. I wanted to be as far away from there as I could.

One of the girls who couldn't have been much older than I am came out onto the porch and put her arms around me. I wanted to ask her why she was there and how she became what she is but I suppose people could ask me the same thing and I wouldn't be able to give them a simple answer. A year ago, two years ago, I could have told any-body anything. Ask me a question and I knew the answer. Now it seems like I don't know anything and I'm seventeen.

"Come inside," the girl said after awhile. "It's getting cold out here."

"Yes, I guess it is," I said.

We sat on one of the over-stuffed couches, listening to the laughter that came from the other rooms. We were all alone. Even the Yanks' bodies had been taken out of the room. I don't know where.

Some of the men had laughed at me for not wanting to sleep with any of the girls (some of them were really girls) earlier that day. One of them had even asked if I was yellow.

I said, "Do I look like I'm afraid?"

He said, "You look like someone who thinks he should stick his pecker in a knothole."

He was laughing when I cocked my pistol, sticking the barrel into his left nostril. Suddenly the whole place was quiet and it was almost like he was dangling there on the end of my pistol. He sputtered so hard his whole body began to convulse and I thought he was going to throw up, so I holstered my gun.

Anderson said, "He was just tryin' to be funny, Jess," but it wasn't true.

Some men think they have to have sex with any woman who's available or they aren't men, and I guess he was one of them.

The girl I was sitting with said, "Would you like me? We could go into my room."

She wore a blue dress and she had the clearest blue eyes I've ever seen. She hardly wore any make-up and, if I'd had ten guesses, I wouldn't have guessed what her profession was.

I said, "I like you, but I don't want it to be like this."

"Is there someone back home?"

I thought about Zee and how I'd run away to see her one Halloween right after her mother died, but Zee wasn't my girl and that was a long time ago.

I said, "No, there isn't anyone special."

"Are you sure you don't want to go with me? I'll be gentle." I think she knew she'd be my first, and she wanted to be kind. Gentle.

"Just hold me," I said. "That's all I want you to do. Hold me."

I guess I fell asleep like that because the next thing I knew it was dark out and some of the boys were yelling to me from the yard.

The girl was still next to me, sleeping.

Outside, the frost was on the pumpkin.

I realized I'd never asked the girl her name, and she'd never told me. I thought about running back into the house to ask her because it suddenly seemed very important but the boys were already riding off and I still had to saddle up my horse and ride after them in the lonely darkness.

Jesse

Scyene, Texas
Christmas Day 1864

Dear Frank,

Probably you were smart not to come here, but I had to get away from the war, at least for awhile. And even though I miss Missouri, it's been good to see Myra Belle Shirley and her family again.

Her mother has retreated into herself. She can look right at you and you have the feeling she doesn't know you're there. I suppose it's one way to cope with losing a son and being run off from a place you love.

And her father's tired. Beaten. When the weather's nice, he just sits on the porch with his feet up on the railing. You can hear him chewing and spitting, chewing and spitting, or sometimes when he doesn't have any tobacco, he just sighs.

Last night Cole and I helped them decorate the tree. When it was done, they lit candles on it and everyone sang "Silent Night, Holy Night," and everything almost seemed "calm" and "bright" as we stood there.

I don't think anyone else noticed, but Cole had his huge arms around Myra Belle (these days she gets mad if you don't refer to her as Belle), his hands on her breasts. I think she took big breaths on purpose as she sang, "Sleep in heavenly peace."

Cole was smiling and his voice joined hers, booming out "heavenly peace," then he whispered something that made Belle blush. You could see the candles burning in Cole's eyes.

Sometimes I think Cole laughs and drinks too much, swearing when he doesn't have to, that he's too casual about the way other people feel, using them, and I worry about him and Belle. But when I see them together like that, I don't know; maybe we should get any happiness we can, where we can.

Sometimes I don't know why I love that man so much. In some ways, he's everything I'm not, everything I don't want to be, but there's something basic about him. Honest. Elemental. I know he'd never betray a friend. You can trust him. You don't have to look behind your back.

Later on last night I got him alone on the porch (he went out there to smoke a cigar) and said, "Cole, don't do anything to hurt Belle."

He puffed on his cigar for a long time, then he held it between his thumb and index finger, standing there like a politician ready to have his picture taken. He said, "Jesse, learn to lighten up. Have some fun. I know your father was a minister, but you can't spend all your time thinking about going to hell."

"Sometimes I just feel so lost," I said, gesturing at nothing, my arm curving like a gull flying in the dark. "I don't really feel gown-up, but none of us are kids now. I don't know who I am."

"Hell, you sound like Frank. Trying to philosophize. Come on, let's drink and fuck and have some fun."

"Yeah, fun."

When we went back inside, Belle was still fighting the war. She said, "It doesn't matter who wins it. I'll never kiss some Yank's ass." It surprised me to hear her swear.

Cole paced back and forth, his footsteps heavy-sounding on the floor. The boards shook and, as he spoke, his voice got louder and louder. "The goddamn Yanks run everything now, and the war isn't even over yet. Next thing you know, they'll be telling us how to live. Holding a gun between our eyes. Next thing you know we'll have to ask permission to piss, like kids in school."

Belle said, "I'll piss on their foot and say it's raining if I want to."

"I have a gun of my own," Cole said, "and the Yanks aren't the only ones who know how to point. I tell you, I'd like to get some goddamn Yankee banker in my sights and pull the trigger.

"That son-of-a-bitch at the Liberty bank would have a hole where his belly button used to be if it were up to me. I went in there to get change for a hundred dollar bill and Bird looked at me like I was something dirty. He said, 'Where did you get that? I see men like you all the time. Drifters. Riff-raff. You've never worked a day in your life.' Greenup Bird should talk about work. The only place he has a callus is on his ass."

Belle put her arms around Cole and the tips of her fingers barely touched by the time they circled his chest. She said, "In a few minutes it'll be Christmas, and we ought to be rejoicing. There's plenty of time to fight the Yanks."

I know Pa left for California when I was only three, but I still remember that last Christmas he was with us. At least I think I remember, and that's just as good. Maybe better, 'cause I can have it my way. He and Ma and you and I stood around the tree and little Susan was lying in her crib.

I think Ma and Pa were singing "Silent Night, Holy Night," and maybe you were, but I was too little to know the words so I just stood there with my mouth open, pretending to sing.

I thought about that after I'd said goodnight to Cole and Belle. Then I blew out the candles, one by one, until there was only one left. If it had been the evening star, I'd have made a wish, but it wasn't a star so I blew it out, too. Anyway, it was too late for wishes.

Jesse

Kearney, Missouri
June 7, 1865

Dear Zee,

It's over.

Quantrill was killed early in May in Kentucky. I heard he was half-crazy at the end. He was going to take some men to Washington so he could assassinate President Lincoln, turning the Union victory into defeat.

Some of the men who were with him at the end say he foamed at the mouth like a mad dog and all he could do was curse the nigras and the Jayhawkers.

Todd's dead, too. And Anderson.

Everyone's dead, it seems, and I often lay awake at night wondering why I'm alive. Maybe it would be better if I weren't because I have absolutely no idea what I'm going to do. I don't think I can become a farmer, settling down after everything I've been through.

When Lee surrendered, I told myself he'd betrayed the Confederacy, that the war wasn't over yet, but then Taylor gave up too; when General Kirby-Smith surrendered in Texas, I knew it was really over. We were through.

The Union papers like to say how the guerrilla soldiers raped and pillaged, but I never saw a woman raped and the only real pillaging that took place was at Lawrence, and Quantrill was just getting back at the people who'd used it as a base to raid and kill Missourians.

Last month Cole Younger and Frank and I got together.

"Where'll we go?" Cole asked.

I stared into the fire we'd built, wishing I could see into the future. Probably I should be glad I can't. I said, "Maybe we could go back to Texas or drift down into Mexico."

"I don't know," Cole said. "I can't imagine spending the rest of my life hanging around a cantina with a bunch of grease balls in serapes."

"Why shift about in search of unseen lands heated by other suns?" Frank said. "Who, exile bound, escapes himself as well?"

"What the hell does that mean?" Cole asked.

"I read it someplace."

"What does it mean?"

"You can't run away from your troubles, I guess."

"Then why didn't you say that?"

You know Frank. Always reading a book. If there's a fancy way to say something simple he'll find it.

"I liked the sound of it," Frank said. "It's like a poem. We'll need to hang onto everything we can to get through."

"We'll need more than poetry to turn our lives around."

"Well," I said, "we still haven't answered the big question. What are we going to do?"

"I don't know," Frank said. "I guess we'll go home and get on with our lives."

I keep telling myself this is a new beginning for us but each night I sit on the porch, exhausted, and listen to the earth humming. Last night Ma asked if I was all right and I said, "Yeah, I'm fine," but I was lying.

I know it's over. It's all over. Over. But I'll never surrender.

Jesse

Rulo, Nebraska
July 1865

Dear Susan,

Frank and I were riding into Lexington, beneath a white flag, to receive amnesty when the blue bellies fired on us.

One of the bullets hit me in the chest, inches from the wound I got less than a year ago during the war. The impact of the slug almost knocked me from my horse and I looked at Frank and said, "The dirty bastards — shooting at us when we're coming in to surrender. I think they've killed me." But I was wrong.

Frank and I spurred our horses into the woods and, somehow, we lost the blue bellies. That night the moon burned like kerosene. I remember Frank talked to me all night, but I don't remember much of what he said. It was mainly things like, "We'll get even with them, Jesse. We won't let them get away with shooting us down like outlaws. " I think he kept talking because he didn't know what else to do. Maybe he thought I'd die if I didn't have the sound of his voice to keep me alive. Maybe, in a funny way, I did die that night.

We were next to a creek and I kept splashing water onto my wound, bathing it. I kept thinking I was going to black out so I decided to recite all the prayers I knew but I could never get farther than "Our Father Who art in Heaven." I couldn't remember what came after that so I'd start over, "Our Father Who art in Heaven" while I splashed water on myself, but I couldn't find the words, couldn't make the connections. I kept seeing Dr. Samuel that afternoon the Yankees rode into our yard. I guess that's because that was the day it all began for me.

I kept seeing his face turn purple as the blue bellies hung him from the coffee bean tree behind our house. They wanted him to tell them where Frank was, where Quantrill was hiding, and when he wouldn't they'd lift him off the ground, laughing, "Look at that Reb dance." He was a tired old man.

You remember. I tried to stop them, "Our Father Who art in Heaven... Who art... our Father," but they tied me to the tree and began whipping me. "This'll teach you to interfere." And Ma was screaming, rocking Dr. Samuel back and forth, his face the color of a plum, but after they'd lashed me a couple of times I couldn't hear anything but the whip. "Our Father Who art... our Father." The whip cut through the air, swish, like the Reaper's scythe, and it made a dull kind of fup sound when it hit me and I could feel the blood running down my back... the blood.

I tried to stop the bleeding while I stood there in the creek bathing my wound, tried to hold back the hate I felt. I didn't want to hate anyone, not even the blue bellies, but they shot me. SHOT ME. And the war was over. And we were supposed to get on with our lives. And they'd promised me. Promises.

I was still bleeding, but it had slowed down some, when Frank and I rode across a field. There was a farmer there, plowing, and Frank said, "Mister, we need your help. You got to... you got to," and the farmer said something I couldn't understand, "Our Father... father... we never saw," then the sky turned upside down and the plowed furrows that looked like a pomegranate someone had split open and stepped on came up to meet me and then there was nothing.

Jesse

14

Harlem, Missouri
August 2, 1865

Dear Susan,

Cousin Zee has been taking care of me since I arrived here. She has long dark hair, which she often wears in a bun; when she does that, it gives her a stern look, so I told her, "Zee, let your hair down when you're with me."

"I'd be embarrassed," she said, laughing. She laughs often, blushing, her face a pink rose.

"You look so beautiful with your hair down."

"Jesse, you'll go to hell for lying."

She loves to watch me. I don't mind that when I'm shaving or reading the Bible to her, but we're both nervous when I have to pee. I'm not strong enough to stand for more than a few seconds yet, so I swing my feet over the edge of the bed, just touching the floor with them. Even that little effort takes my breath away. I break out sweating when I feel the pain in my chest.

Zee holds the pot, looking the other way, although I can tell she wants to watch me.

I remember the way you'd watch when I'd pee in the loft, and my urine would stream down onto the ground. Once you said, "It's like a golden waterfall. I wish I could do that." It was the first time I realized how different men and women are. I remember you wanted to touch it, it was so new and strange to you—beautiful—but I didn't think you should.

Zee's hands shook so badly the first time she held the pot that I didn't think I'd be able to hit it. "Don't be nervous," I said.

"I shouldn't be doing this."

"Someone has to or there'll be a mess."

She was so rigid I had trouble going by the time she steadied herself.

I sighed when I began peeing. Zee started to shake again and I told her, "Don't think about this. Just pretend it's raining."

"Raining?"

"Yes. The rain's falling onto a tin roof. Can't you hear it?"

She seemed almost dreamy then. "Yes, I hear it."

I remember the way my urine sounded when it hit the straw that afternoon with you. It seemed to sizzle.

Raining.

When I finished, Zee took the pot away, then she helped me swing my legs back up onto the bed. I don't think I ever did a harder day's work.

I'm stronger now. Yesterday I joined the family for dinner for the first time. Dr. Samuel's sister and our aunt served the food and when they asked me to say grace I said, "When thou makest a feast, call the poor, the maimed, the lame, the blind: And thou shall be blessed."

Before we started to eat I said, "I may not be poor, but I'm sure maimed and lame. If I were a horse they'd put a bullet in my brain."

Sometimes my headaches are so bad I think a bullet in my brain might be the only way to stop them, but I just take some more morphine and go back to bed.

When I awaken, the headaches generally aren't so intense.

Now, if I could just stop dreaming.

I miss you.

Jesse

Harlem, Missouri
September 10, 1865

Dear Susan.

I dream about you.

In one of the dreams we're little kids, playing in the back yard. We're making figures in the dirt with sticks and Ma's chickens are pecking at the corn she threw out for them.

Suddenly, one of the chickens comes toward you, flapping its wings and pecking at your face even though you haven't done anything. You've hardly moved.

I yell for it to go away, but it won't leave.

It begins pecking at your cheek and when I grab the chicken, there's blood on my hand. When I see that, I begin crying, shouting for Ma, "Help us, help us," but she doesn't hear me. No one hears me and the chicken's pecking at you again so I grab it by its neck, twisting. It's squawking, pecking at me now. I can't twist hard enough to kill it so I... I stick the chicken's head into my mouth, biting down as hard as I can. Then, all of a sudden, I drop its headless body to the ground and spit out feathers and... and blood... and the head of the chicken... and I begin to vomit because all I can taste is feathers and blood. I say, "I've never killed anything before."

I almost go crazy, running toward the other chickens, kicking at them and screaming until you grab me, putting your arms around me.

You lead me over to the back steps and force me to sit. You have your arm around me and... I've never felt closer to you. I'm aware of you in a way I've never been before, and I'll never see you quite the same way again.

I'm crying and spitting and you're trying to rock me, almost singing to me when you talk.

I try to say something but I can't get the words out because of the blood... and the feathers... and the dust in the yard. The dust is swirling and I keep blinking my eyes furiously... so I can see. Everything is out of focus... the way it is when I've taken too much morphine to dull the pain in my chest.

You're looking at me, your pupils huge, the way they'd be in the dark, but it's the middle of the afternoon.

"I had to do it," I say. "That chicken was going to peck your eyes out."

"It's all right," you say. "It's all right."

"No, it isn't. It isn't. It'll never be all right," I say, and it hasn't been.

I'm dying here.

I want to come home.

Your loving brother,
Jesse

Harlem
September 15, 1865

Dear Frank,

I worry about being fast enough with a gun since I was wounded.

Lately, I've stood in front of the large mirror hanging at one end of the hall and practiced drawing my pistol. At first it took me five seconds or so to get my pistol out of the holster, but then I got it down to four, to three, and I started to feel more in touch with my real self again. But I kept remembering the time when I could draw my pistol in a second or less—no one was faster than me—and I'd stand in front of the mirror, practicing my draw for an hour or two.

My arm would get sore and sweat would run down into my eyes until my image blurred. I'd draw my pistol while I was coming up, fast, from a crouch or rolling over, trying to get my pistol out of the holster, my shoulder hitting the wall. Sometimes I'd stand in front of the mirror as if I were facing someone in the street. Sometimes I'd turn, as if someone behind me had suddenly called my name, "Jesse," and I'd shoot from the hip.

One day, I became so involved with practicing my draw that I forgot I was pretending and I fired my pistol, the shot echoing in the hall.

The mirror broke into a thousand shards and when I saw my jagged life reflected back at me, I almost cried.

I said, "You've killed yourself, you've killed yourself," and it took a few moments to realize I was still alive.

Jesse

18

Harlem
September 21, 1865

Dear Susan,

Women who are born on this day are often referred to as the last rose of summer. I've always wished your birthday fell on the twenty-first (no matter, you'll always be my last rose—and my first) although I loved it when we celebrated your birthday on Thanksgiving. Right now, lying here in pain much of the time, it's hard to be thankful for anything, although Zee's taking good care of me; and each day I feel myself getting stronger.

When I was moved from Lexington to Rulo, I thought I was going to be jolted to death, even though Frank laid me on a bed of straw in the wagon. When I was conscious, I'd lie on my back, looking up at the high porcelain sky, dreaming: I was coming home. But Rulo wasn't Kearney and neither is Harlem, although I'm happier here. And now I know I'm not going to die. Not for awhile yet. Unless it's from boredom.

Zee does what she can for me. Yesterday we went for a walk to the river. A minister there was baptizing some darkies. Their faces were so black they kind of looked like large rotten apples except for the whites of their eyes and their teeth and every time the preacher would push one under he'd shout, "Hallelujah!" The afternoon just rang with hallelujahs. And when the darkie would come out of the water the preacher would shout "Amen" and all the darkies would start shouting with him, making a chorus, and I tell you, I never heard so many hallelujahs and amens in one afternoon.

I told myself it must be wonderful to be able to love something so much, then I thought of you and the baptisms we'd witnessed and the way we'd play, pretend. Sometimes I'd be the minister and sometimes you would. I remember how mad Ma got the time you came home wet. I'd push you under the water and you'd come up spluttering, your wet hair the color of the sun, then I'd push you down again and

you'd come up laughing. "Jesse," you'd say, all breathless.
I loved watching you.

When I told Ma what we'd been doing she said we were
mocking the Lord, but I thought not; I said, "I don't believe
there's only one way to honor Him, do you?" and I could
tell she had to think about it. She never did answer me.

I tried to tell Zee about the times we had, but after
awhile she just put her finger to my lips and said, "Shush,
Jesse, shush," as if I were a child. Maybe that's what I've
seemed like to her. I'm only 18, but she'll never understand
the killing I've seen. Never understand the way it can numb
you, no matter how much you fight against it. But she's a
good woman and when she put her arm around me, I kind of
shivered.

When we went back to the house, Zee rubbed witch
hazel onto my chest and I started to tell her how you used to
rub my back with myrtle oil but, for some reason, I didn't. I
just lay there, feeling her hands, thinking they were yours. I
remembered you asked me if I knew myrtle oil was used as
an emblem of love in ancient days; Venus held it sacred.
You whispered as if it were a secret you didn't want anyone
else to share but us. Maybe that's why I didn't say anything
to Zee.

Just before I fell asleep, tired from the walk and the sun
and the morphine, I said, "I love the way your hands feel,
Susan," and I felt Zee stiffen.

She said, "It's *me*, Jesse. Your cousin Zee. *I'm* the one
with you. *Zee*." Then she began to knead me again and I
nodded and said something I don't remember and fell
asleep.

Love,
Jesse

Harlem
late September 1865

Dear Susan,

I keep dreaming about you.

When I'm taking a lot of morphine, the dreams are more frequent, more vivid, and I see everything in color.

Normally, I dream in black and white.

In the dream I had last night we must have been in our early teens.

You climbed up to a hayloft, ahead of me, and I could see your underpants, white as a cloud, beneath your red dress.

We sat in the loft, looking out over the fields at the snow, and I felt like my skin was on fire, maybe because of the straw, I don't know, but I was suddenly nervous. I wanted to get out of there, and I asked if you'd like to go sled riding with me.

We took the toboggan to the top of the hill behind the house, and I remember the sun was going down.

You said, "The daylight's burning away, the way our lives do," and I thought it was a strange thing for someone so young to say, especially you; I was always the one with the strong sense of mortality, of time passing us by.

You put your arms around me and we pushed off, going down the hill faster and faster. It felt like we were out of control and I think you were screaming, or maybe it was just the wind in my ears. I don't know.

The toboggan turned over before we reached the foot of the hill and we rolled through the snow, holding on to each other.

When we stopped you said, "I could feel your hands on me, everywhere."

Then neither of us said anything.

You were underneath me but both of us were breathing hard. I could feel your breasts rising and falling, even through our clothes. Rising and falling. I remember sitting up to brush the snow off myself. You were still lying in the

snow and I couldn't stop looking at the way your breasts
heaved even though I felt there was... something wrong
about it. That I shouldn't be looking like that.

You said, "They're bigger than most girls' my age,
don't you think?" and I pretended I didn't hear you.

"Don't you think they're bigger?"

"You shouldn't talk like that," I said.

"Why not?"

"I... I don't know." (I'm not sure that I know now.)
"Because you're my sister, I guess."

"Does that mean it's wrong for you to look at me?"

Then you sat up, pulling my head to your breasts and I
remember closing my eyes so tightly they hurt and all I
could see was red through my eyelids. I could hear the
sound of your heart and I wanted to... I wanted to... do
something I don't want to think about.

But I can't help what I dream. Can I?

Jesse

Kearney
Thanksgiving 1865

Dear Zee,

Susan says I love you because of the family resemblance,
that when I look at you it's like I'm looking at myself.

"It's like Narcissus looking into the fountain."

"Who was Narcissus?" I asked.

"Someone from ancient times noted for his beauty."

Susan said that Narcissus saw his reflection in water
and fell in love with it. He thought his reflection was actually
another person, the presiding nymph of the place.

"What's a nymph?" I asked.

"Well, a nymph is... I don't know... a minor god in Greek
mythology or something. Just let me tell you the story. "

Susan didn't say this but, apparently, nymphs aren't
very smart.

It seems that Narcissus pined away for this spirit he thought he saw and, finally, he jumped into the fountain and died.

"That's a stupid story," I said.

"Other nymphs came for his body so they could have a funeral for Narcissus but they just found a flower there so they named it after him."

"The last time I saw myself in the mirror I killed myself. So much for my good looks," I told Susan, and she looked as if she thought I was crazy. Then I told her how I shot the mirror in your hall.

When you came to see what happened, I was on my hands and knees trying to pick up the pieces of glass, my ears ringing, my hands bleeding.

"Jesse, are you all right?" you asked.

"No, I've just killed myself," I said, wiping my bloody hands on my face and my white shirt. Blood-soaked pieces of mirror were all over the floor and I could see an eyeball here and a finger there and a piece of my arm somewhere else and I began to sob. "Dammit, Zee, I'm too young to die."

I told Susan that you sat on the floor next to me, putting your arms around me. You said, "I'll take care of you. I won't let you die, Jesse. I'll never let you die," and for a moment you almost made me believe everything would be all right.

Next spring when I see a narcissus, I'll pick the most delicate one I can find and bring it to you with a message: I want you to be mine.

Jesse

Kearney
December 26, 1865

Dear Cole,

I proposed to Zee yesterday and she said she'd marry

me. We were sitting at the foot of the huge spruce tree we'd decorated for Christmas and the smell of the tree and the candy being made in the kitchen filled the house and I don't know that I've ever been happier.

I'd been reading Dickens' *Christmas Carol* to her while she lay on the floor, her head on my lap, and I told Zee I feel like an unredeemed Scrooge except for those moments I'm with her.

I am unredeemed. I was even rebaptized at the New Hope Baptist Church, the one my father was pastor at, in an attempt to leave the war behind but I can't forget it, maybe because I don't want to. At least I was alive then.

Now, each day is pretty much the same. At dawn I'm out in the field, plowing. I have blisters on my hands, my back aches and my butt feels like I rode a mule a hundred miles. Bareback.

Is this what we fought the war for?

Sometimes I think I'd like to spread the word of God, becoming a minister like the father I never knew. He left for California when I was three. He never came back, although we were told he died in the gold fields there. The last letter Ma received said he could take consolation that, through the art of writing, he could converse as if "face to face." I understand that, although I sometimes think I'm writing most of my letters to myself. I keep hoping I'll find out who I am.

Ma says I'll never make a good preacher, and she's probably right. If my parishioners didn't get "the word" I'd probably stick a gun in their face and say, "Look at God." Sometimes I don't think I know how to live without violence anymore.

Sometimes, Frank and I ride into Liberty, spurring our horses at full gallop, racing back and forth up the streets, hurrahing people (I hate myself later) because we don't know what else to do. Sometimes I'll even fire my pistol because I don't want to forget what a gunshot sounds like.

I know it's wrong, but sometimes I think I want to die.

That maybe I'd have been better off if I'd died from my wounds. Maybe I should even have been one of those Yanks you tried your Enfield rifle on. I can still see the sun glinting from your red hair, your mouth open, laughing. The spurts of blood on the blue of those Yanks' uniforms each time you fired. It was like roses blossomed from their chests . When I tell Zee about it, she trembles and says, "Coleman Younger must be a terrible man. You should forget about people like that."

"At least I was alive then."

"You're alive now."

"Most of the time I'm just pretending. I go through the motions."

"Are you pretending now?"

We'd gone into the kitchen and I was cranking the handle to make ice cream. I could feel the tiredness setting in, but it wasn't the good tiredness we had after a battle with the blue bellies. It was something else. Numbing. Insidious. It creeps in on you like the night.

Zee asked, "Are you happy now?"

It was almost dusk and my arm and my chest ached and I knew I'd have to take some morphine to make it through dinner, but I kept turning the crank: bored, bored, bored. What kind of a husband will I make? Cranking. Going through the motions.

"I've never be happier," I said.

Happy New Year,
Jesse

Kearney
St. Valentine's Day 1866

Dear Belle,

Cole says he wishes you could have been with us yesterday.

We rode into Liberty, with eight other men, about two

in the afternoon. When we approached the square, the Confederate flag was flying (the blue bellies haven't ripped it down yet) from the courthouse. We wore long blue overcoats and my lips froze to my muffler, ripping the skin away when I took it off, and you could see our horses' breath in the air.

My teeth ached from the cold. I felt like I could bite the frozen air and crack the sky.

You could feel the snow coming. It was going to be a blizzard.

"I haven't felt this alive since the war," Cole said.

The men with us were riding around the square, hurrahing, firing their pistols to keep people off the streets; but there weren't many there, even when we rode in, because of the cold. Spit froze before it hit the ground. You could hear the gunshots and the horses' hooves striking the cobblestones.

Cole and I dismounted in front of the National Bank and I felt my boots slip on the ice as we went inside. Cole has never forgotten the argument he had with Greenup Bird, but it's more than that.

The bankers have prospered on the blood of the Confederacy, on the dying, on the oppressed, on the labor of the small farmer who's charged rates of interest that drive him into bankruptcy. You know how many hard-working, honest men we've seen lose farms they've had for years. If they aren't stolen by Carpetbaggers, they're stolen by the bankers. "Which is worse," people ask, "a blue belly or a banker?" It's a riddle that doesn't have an answer. But these days people around here spit when they see a banker go by. "What else can we do?" they ask, watching everything they've worked for disappear.

Yesterday we showed them what they can do.

Cole and I stood by the stove near the bank windows for a moment, rubbing our hands together, then he went over to the cashier's desk. Bird's son, William, was there.

Outside, it was beginning to snow. Softly. The flakes swirled down like they were caught in a vortex.

"Remember me?" Cole asked.

"No, sir."

"Maybe your pa does."

Cole's voice was white with rage and I think both Birds knew something was wrong. Cole said, "Do you think you can change a hundred dollar bill for me? Do you?"

William hesitated, looking at his father.

I could hear gunshots out on the street, but it was hard to see much because the snow was coming down harder now.

Cole pulled his pistol and said, "Forget the hundred. I want all the money in the damn bank, and I want it fast."

I pulled my gun, too, moving toward the Birds so quickly that I felt a sharp pain in my chest. I caught my breath, dizzy, and for a second I thought it was snowing in the bank. There were spots swirling in front of me.

We shoved both men into the vault and watched them put the money into the grain sacks we had under our coats. "Fill them up and don't say a word," I told them, "or it'll be your last."

"You... you won't get away with this," Greenup said.

"If we don't," Cole smiled, "you won't be around to know about it."

I blinked my eyes rapidly, trying to make the snow go away.

"My hand's starting to shake," I said, "and if it shakes too much this pistol's going to go off—in your face," and I watched Greenup sweat. It was the best I'd felt in a long time. Finally, we were standing up. We were saying: First you tried to kill us, then you tried to take our pride away. But we're not going to let you. You can only push us around so much.

Cole stuck his face into Greenup's and asked, "Are you sure you don't remember me?"

"I'm positive."

"Well, I want you to remember me this time. I don't ever want you to forget." Cole cocked his pistol, sticking it into Greenup's ear.

"I don't want to die."

"Neither do those people who lost their farms to the bank," Cole said. "Just keep shoveling the money into those sacks."

When they were filled, Cole and I backed out of the vault. Just before he slammed the door, Cole said, "Birds like you ought to be locked up," then he laughed in a way I hadn't heard him since Texas. What a long, bloody road it's been.

As we rode out of town with the rest of the boys, we all fired our guns and I saw someone go down. But maybe he fell on the ice. I don't know. I hate killing, but something in you goes numb when you see enough men die. You get hard. Inured. Sometimes I think it's a miracle any man who's been to war can fall in love, but I've done it. And I know Cole has.

When we got to the river south of town, we crossed it on a ferry. We weren't far ahead of a posse that had been formed, but by the time we got across the river the snow had really begun to come down. We'd lose anyone following us.

"The damn fools," Cole said. "They ought to be applauding us, not out to get us. Most of them owe the bankers money."

We had almost $60,000 in our grain sacks.

I could barely see Cole a few feet ahead of me. I kept rubbing my eyes, looking down to avoid the glare, but the ground was white too. Everything was white.

I don't know when the posse turned back.

It was so quiet it was eerie. There was just the flop, flup of our horses' hooves. It was like they were stepping on cotton. The sky cracking. Everything giving way.

I felt like I was going to disappear into the snow, felt like I was going to be sucked into the whiteness and that I was going to come out in some place I'd never been before, where the war and everything else that was painful would be behind me.

Jesse

Brandenburg, Kentucky
July 10, 1866

Dear Ma,

All Frank talks about is coming home.

He walks with a cane, limping badly, but he's better off than three of the blue bellies who ambushed him here. He was hit in the hip, but he killed two of the men who shot him and he wounded a third.

The strange thing is, he doesn't even know why they did it. Maybe winning the war wasn't enough for them. Maybe they want us to suffer forever. Stepping on others makes weak men feel strong. But they tried to step on the wrong person when they shot at Frank.

We took a short walk down to the Ohio River today. Across the river, the sun was shining in Indiana, but it was hazy and humid on the Kentucky side.

"It's like the story of our lives," Frank said. "We're always on the wrong side."

"We were on the right side. We just lost."

The wind came up, ruffling the surface of the water, like someone was skipping invisible stones over its surface, and the leaves in the trees almost made a clattering sound. It gave me a lonely feeling, even though I was with Frank.

"I want to go home, Jesse.

"Not yet. You're not able to travel yet. Pretty soon."

I remember how badly I wanted to go home after I was ambushed at Lexington, but I thought I was dying and Frank isn't. I've told him that. Told him a lot of people have been shot up worse than him but he says, "That doesn't make me feel any better. Knowing someone else might have lost a leg doesn't make the wound in my hip hurt any less. Doesn't make me any less anxious to get back to Missouri. Someone else's pain doesn't diminish mine."

Frank, the philosopher. At times he makes me feel like a fool. He can be so damned logical.

The leaves were rattling like castanets in the rising wind. You could feel the rain coming. Up river, lightning broke the sky like a saber and the sky turned green.

"We'd better get back," I said. "We'll get soaked if we stay here much longer."

"Maybe the rain will wash away our sins," Frank said. I couldn't tell if he was joking or not.

I said, "I thought it took the blood of the lamb to do that," just as the sky split apart and we walked back to where we were staying in the green rain.

Love,
Jesse

Nashville, Tennessee
March 1867

Dear Belle,

Blue bellies are everywhere.

They say I'm an outlaw, although I never ambushed them.

They aren't the ones whose lives are threatened almost daily. They aren't the ones who are being forced off their land. They're not the ones who have to make sure they're heavily armed everywhere they go. (I carry two pistols with me when I plow.) They're not the ones who are bleeding. At night I still hemorrhage from the wounds I received. In the mornings, often, my sheets are red.

I cough up my lungs, gasping. Doctors here say I'm dying and I ought to go to California.

On the night of February 18th, five men, well armed and mounted, came to my mother's house.

The weather was so cold the windows were iced up and I was in bed, scarcely able to get up. My wounds had hurt me all day and I'd taken some morphine. I told myself I had to get my guns, which I always kept beside me, but it was seconds before I reached out for them. Long seconds. I could hear the clock ticking. Could hear men's voices a long ways off. "Let us in. *Now*." They banged on the door.

Dr. Samuel heard them walk up onto the porch and he

yelled, "What do you want?" I could hear him faintly.

I was still reaching, trying to grab my pistols. My chest ached. It was hard to breathe. I could see my hand moving slowly. It was like watching a crippled person trying to walk across a room. Maddening. I watched my index finger touch one of the pistols. It gleamed in the opaque light coming in the window.

There was more banging. "Let us in."

Dr. Samuel came up to my room. I don't think I'd seen him look so old, so frail, since the day the Yanks strung him up in our yard. He looked green in the light and his skin hung on him. He asked, "What'll we do, Jesse? What'll I tell them?"

"Tell them to go to hell," I said.

He helped me over to the window. I had to scrape the ice off the glass with my nails; when I looked out, it was like trying to see through a spider web because there was still ice on the window. There was snow on the ground and the moon was shining.

I saw that the horses hitched to the fence all had on cavalry saddles so then I knew; the men were soldiers.

"We know Jesse's in there, and you'd better let us have him if you know what's good for you." Then they began beating on the door with the butts of their rifles. "Goddamn it, James, you'd better come out of there."

I went down the stairs softly. Slowly. Right foot. Left foot. Right. Left. Some of the stairs squeaked, but no one would hear them because of the yelling outside.

I had a pistol in each hand and I got up close to the door, listening to the men talk so I could get a pretty good idea of where they were.

Then, putting my pistol up to within about three inches of the upper panel, I fired.

One of the men screamed, "Goddamn it, the son-of-a-bitch shot me," then I could hear a body hitting the porch.

The gunpowder scorched my nose and I was half-blind for a couple of seconds because of the flash from the gun. I didn't even feel the splinters from the door that had gone into the back of my hand until later.

Before the surprise wore off, I threw the door wide open and began firing with both pistols. I pulled the triggers as fast as I could, but it seemed to take a long time between shots. Bang... bang... It was like listening to a shade flap in a dead breeze. You can wait for minutes for it to be lifted up and then fall back again, hitting the sill. But I must have been firing faster than that.

I hit one of the men as he was running across the yard and two others didn't make it to their horses.

"So you wanted me, huh?" I screamed. "Here I am, you Yankee bastards!"

I'd surprised them so completely that no one had fired a shot at me, and I watched the last man mount his horse. I knew they would have murdered me in my bed or strung me up but, somehow, I didn't care if he got away or not. I was beginning to feel the powder burn and the splinters and I noticed my hand was bleeding, but I didn't care about that either. I didn't even feel good about the men I'd shot. I suddenly felt sick, tired, but I knew I had to get out of there because more soldiers would be back.

Ma had come out onto the porch and I put an arm around her. "I've got to go."

"I know." That was all she said. "I know."

She went into the kitchen, getting me some food, while Dr. Samuel saddled my horse.

It seems like I'm always leaving home.

When I rode away, the sky was the color of a robin's breast, but the sun came up like a broken egg, yellow and rotten, and I rode, hunched over, into the anemic dawn.

Jesse

Scyene, Texas
June 2, 1868

Dear Zee,

I saw a bird once.

It flew into a window, hitting it again and again until it fell to the ground, exhausted, and died there.

Even if I wanted to, the Yanks wouldn't let me teach school. (Can you imagine me a school teacher?) They wouldn't let me run for public office, not even in my home state. They wouldn't let me preach a sermon.

What am I supposed to do?

I'm that bird, battering my body against the window. But I'm not as easy to kill.

You've asked me why I keep shotguns and pistols in every room of my house. Asked me why I'm gone for days at a time. And why I own the best horses in the state since I don't race them.

I think you know the answer. You just don't want to face it. But if we're going to make it together, you have to.

Sometimes I've wanted to shake you and say, "What do you think I do?"

Well?

Two weeks ago, Frank, Cole, Jim and I rode into Russellville, Kentucky.

We reined our horses in front of the Long & Norton Bank, flipping a coin to see who'd go inside and who'd stay with the horses. Cole and I said heads and when the coin landed in the dust, it was our call.

Inside, Long stood behind the teller's cage and a clerk sat at a desk. Cole handed Long a hundred dollar bill and said, "I'd like you to change this, please."

I know you don't care much for Cole, but you know how polite he can be.

Long looked at the bill, crinkling it between his fingers. Then he even smelled it. For a minute, I thought he was going to take a bite out of it to see how it tasted, but he didn't.

He said, "I'm sorry. This bill is counterfeit."

"I guess it is," Cole said smiling, "but this isn't," and he pulled his revolver, aiming it at Long. "Open the vault."

Long got as blanched looking as a turnip but instead of opening the vault, the fool started to scream. "The bank's being robbed." And then he ran toward the rear exit.

Cole fired a quick shot that grazed him, but Long made it out the door. We could still hear him screaming from the street. Out front, Jim and Frank were looking in five directions at once, trying to keep the horses steady.

"OK, *you*," I said, pointing my pistol at the clerk. "Open the vault if you want to stay alive." I was going to tell him I needed the money for a trip west, for my health, but I didn't think he'd care. That's the trouble with people, Zee. It's an uncaring world. I could live or die and it wouldn't matter to anyone. Well, maybe to you and a few others, but I'm not even sure of that.

The clerk opened the vault and Cole and I stuffed $14,000 worth of gold, silver and greenbacks into the grain sack we carried with us, then we ran out into the street.

At the far end there were some men yelling things we couldn't make out, but we didn't want to hang around to find out what they were saying.

"I thought you boys must have stayed to have a cup of coffee," Frank said. "You took long enough."

About forty men must have been trailing us by a quarter mile as we spurred our horses past the edge of town. But I had a feeling they were just going through the motions. Doing their duty. They didn't really want to get too close to us.

None of them even fired a shot, and neither did we. That's the best way: no one gets hurt.

About five miles out of town, we entered a grove of trees and Cole said, "I think we've lost them."

"Yeah, I said, "but I don't think I'll stop looking behind me for awhile yet."

"Hell, they're probably as relieved as we are," Frank said. "We can take it easy now."

"Not me," I said and I spurred my horse—hard—and headed west toward Texas.

Now. Don't ever ask me what I do again.

Love,
Jesse

Scyene
June 3, 1868

Dear Susan,

We came here to see a man named Gonzales.

He's a skinny little guy who doesn't have the swarthy complexion most Mexicans do. His skin is kind of yellow, like he ate too many bananas.

When we met Gonzales a few years back, he said he could convert gold to greenbacks for us if we ever needed his help. Well, Cole remembered that, even though we never thought we'd need Gonzales' services at the time. The one thing Gonzales didn't tell us was how much he'd charge. But we found out.

When I went into the cantina, he and Cole were arguing. Cole looked at me and said, "This stinking greaser wants a forty percent cut."

Gonzales just smiled and shrugged. He was drinking a beer with a lot of foam on top and it made him look like he had a white mustache. He said, "Watch who you call names, gringo. You're not in Missouri now."

"I can tell than," Cole said. "No one there would try to pull this kind of crap."

"You don't want to do business, we don't have to do no business," Gonzales said. "You can go elsewhere."

"You heathen bastard. You know there isn't anything between here and Mexico but a few cantinas, some shithouses, a couple of dozen fat whores and a lot of cactus. Where would we take our business?"

Gonzales just shrugged again. And they say Orientals

are inscrutable.

"OK, we'll take the deal," I said, then I got Cole out of there as fast as I could.

He was belly-aching all the way back to Belle's, though, telling me what he thought about Mexicans and how the wrong people had won at the Alamo. Cole said, "It's too bad Crockett and his men didn't kill every spic son-of-a-bitch on this side of the Rio Grande." But he'd calmed down some by the time he finished dinner.

Cole went out on the porch to belch and fart and he must have let his belt out two notches after everything he ate. He smoked one of his terrible smelling cigars while Belle was in the front room playing the piano, and Frank and I walked out onto the prairie.

Tomorrow we'll leave for Uncle Drury's.

Frank said, "Going west will be good for you. You'll come home a new man."

"Yeah, or I won't come home at all."

Frank didn't want to admit to the truth of that and neither did I so we just stood there in the enormous darkness, listening to the piano and the crickets and all the other night sounds.

"You'll be back," Frank said.

"Yeah, what is it they say about bad pennies?"

"You're as good a man as I've ever met."

"Tell that to the people who want me dead."

"They don't know you the way I do," Frank said, then he put his hand on my shoulder as if he were going to tell me the secrets of the universe, something he'd discovered from all those books he reads. But all he said was, "Take care of yourself, *compadre*," then he turned around and walked back toward the house and the light and the music and the world.

Pretty soon I thought I could hear Frank's voice over the sound of the piano. He said, "Jesse's got to be all right."

"He'll be fine," Cole said. "Just fine."

I told myself the same thing but I could feel the pain in

my chest if I sucked in too much of the night air, and my
voice didn't sound nearly as authoritative as Cole's.

Love,
Jesse

Paso Robles, California
June 25, 1868

Dear Zee,

I didn't see a lot of Cole or Belle when we were in
Texas because they were always off by themselves.

They reminded me of us in some ways, although Cole's
louder that I could ever be and sometimes I think he'll never
settle down, never marry, whereas I know you're going to
be my wife. I've probably known it since I was a kid, before
I even knew I knew, and I don't want anyone else.

Cole rides over the hill and there's another woman.

He's like that bear that goes over the mountain to see
what he can see.

The last night I was in Scyene, Belle and I went for a
walk and she asked, "Do you think Cole loves me?"

I didn't want to answer that. "As much as he can love
any woman," I finally said. "He's a hard man. I'm not sure
a woman is necessary to him, the way one is for me. Or
Frank. With Cole, a lot of it's physical."

"He says he wants us to go to the Pacific Northwest
together, but he doesn't have the money yet. Do you believe
him?" Then she asked plaintively, "Where's the Pacific
Northwest?"

"I don't know. Oregon. Washington, I guess."

"Cole says it's always green and that the ocean extends
from here to Missouri, even further. Do you think that's
true?"

"It's a big world, Belle."

She shivered, even though it was warm out, and I gave
her the coat I was wearing.

Belle said, "Sometimes I feel so alone, Jesse. Even when Cole and I are together. It's like a piece of him... isn't there."

"I don't think any of us have been right since the war," I said. "We're..." I searched for a word. "Fragmented, I guess. There's an emptiness inside all of us. Cole. Me. Frank."

"I can ride and shoot better than most men. But I know looks are important to men like Cole." I thought she was going to cry then. "Damn it, I know I'm plain."

"No, you're not. There's something vital about you."

"I'm plain, Jesse. Always have been. Always will be. Face it. How can Cole love someone like me?"

"We love people for a lot of different reasons," I said and I started to count all the reasons I have for loving you but there are too many of them so I stopped counting after awhile.

Belle noticed how quiet I'd become. "What are you thinking about?" she asked.

"I'm just remembering Zee," I said. "I'm always remembering Zee. No matter where I am."

I hope you think of me once in awhile.

Love,
Jesse

Paso Robles
June 28, 1868

Dear Susan,

I've been at Uncle Drury's resort for two weeks now and already I'm feeling better. Stronger. I don't awaken in the middle of the night with my chest constricted, gulping for air. I go down to the sulfur springs each day and I eat lemons and oranges and a pound of fish. Once I even went out to the ocean.

I took my boots off, walking through the sand in my

bare feet. The Pacific was incredibly blue (bluer than the bluest sky we've ever seen in Missouri) and way out toward the horizon I could see what looked like a geyser. I pointed it out and asked Uncle Drury, "What's that?"

"It's a leviathan," he said.

Later, it came closer to shore and I could see its great black hump cresting the waves. It must have been forty feet long and Uncle Drury told me it probably weighs a ton a foot.

In the afternoon I took my clothes off, wading into the water. I could smell the salt and the kelp and I could feel the sun beating down on me as the water lapped at my thighs. I shivered when the waves came up to my genitals. The sand seemed to be moving beneath me and I felt like I was sliding out to sea. It was like skating on sand. Sometimes I'd lose my balance, tumbling into the water, but I didn't mind.

I could feel the salt crystals on my skin when I lay on the beach, sunning myself dry, and I remembered the times we'd go down to the river together and go into the water without our clothes.

I remember when I discovered how to masturbate and I showed you. It was twilight and your eyes got bigger and bigger as you watched me and, finally, your eyes were almost filled with your pupils and the sun's reflection and I could almost imagine I saw what you saw. You said, "You have such a strange expression. What are you feeling?"

"I'm not sure."

You told me my hand seemed to blur I moved it so rapidly. You said, "Jesse, don't hurt yourself," and I just told you to keep watching. And to be quiet.

It got bigger and bigger and then, suddenly, it was as if it burst and I almost cried, my legs shaking. Weak. It was like being wounded, but it was a good feeling. It's the only time I've never minded being vulnerable.

I remember that afternoon in the barn, too. You'd taken Dr. Samuel's stethoscope and you told me you wanted to listen to my heart. I was touching myself, touching, when you put the stethoscope to my chest and said, "I can hear it beating."

"You're not a doctor."

"No, but I can hear things. See things."

I could feel your hair brushing against my chest, and I put a hand on your shoulder to steady myself. You said my heart was going faster and faster, that it was going BOOM BOOM BOOM, almost shattering your ears, just before I finished.

"I thought your heart was going to burst," you whispered. "I don't ever want to hear that again."

"No, I guess not," I said.

"We shouldn't be doing this."

"No, I guess not," I said again. I felt drugged. Stupid. I felt like I was on fire.

You said, "Someone might catch us."

"No. No one will ever catch us." But it didn't matter. That was the last time you ever watched me.

Burn this letter,
Jesse

San Francisco
July 4, 1868

Dear Cole,

I rode a ferry boat today.

It was almost dusk and the light was golden on the water. The hills on either side of the bay seemed burnished.

I stood on the prow so I could feel the wind in my face. I had to hold on to my hat with one hand.

The fog was coming in, but I could see a boat way out toward the Farralone Islands. And I wondered where it was going, where my life is going, and I tried to imagine what it must have been like for Sir Francis Drake and his men when he came here and there was no city. Nothing at all here but the chance for a new life—not many of us get that. Oh God,

I can get melancholy around dusk.

I went into a steambath, sitting there sweating with a towel over my middle. There were a lot of portly, middle aged men there with me. When one of them asked what I did I said, "I'm in the banking business."

"I am too," he said. "I'm manager of a bank here in town. Nothing big yet, but it's growing. Where's your bank?"

"I'm really an investment broker. You know, I travel around. I make a little money here, a little money there. Whatever looks good."

He had an Italian name that was difficult to pronounce, but he said, "Just call me Carlo. Everybody does."

We had a six course dinner at a French restaurant, then we went to a saloon. You know me, I never could drink much, but I won three hundred dollars at roulette. I put an arm around Carlo and said, "Yes, sir, this must be a lucky city for me. Sometime I might have to do business here."

"If I can ever be of help—"

"Well, I'll remember that."

Girls brought customers their drinks. They were wearing ostrich feather hats and red silk jackets and, Cole, the only thing they had on below their jackets were their shoes.

Men kept lifting the jackets up and asking things like, "Is that all you're wearing?"

Most of the women answered, "What does it look like? Do you think I'm wearing a mink there?"

It made me blush, but I couldn't help staring. Life here is a lot different than it is in Kansas City.

One of the women came over to me. I guess she was about our age. She said, "Can I help you?"

"I don't know how." When I told her I already had a beer Carlo laughed so hard he started to choke.

"You really are from the country, aren't you?" he asked. I felt like a fool. I can tell you that. All I wanted to do was get out of there.

When I left—Carlo was still laughing—I walked the

streets of the city and ended up near the marina. They were shooting off fireworks and I stood there watching them. Everyone would ooh and aah each time one exploded and I pretended they were blue and red and green stars.

I thought of how you would have loved those saloon women with their ostrich hats. I could see you putting your hands under their coats, your face as red as their jackets, your voice booming out: "Well, well, well, what have we got here?"

For a moment I thought about going back to the saloon, but it was late by the time the fireworks ended and I was tired and lost in a strange city so I went back to my hotel. I tried to sleep but I was restless, tossing and turning (my chest hurt) so I got up to write this letter. Maybe now I'll be able to sleep.

Jesse

Marysville, California
July 11, 1868

Dear Ma,

I've spent two days looking for Pa's grave, for any sign that he was here, but it's as if he never existed. Sometimes I feel that everyone in the world has a father except Frank, Susie and me, although I know Dr. Samuel has done his best. Still, I'd like to know my "real" Pa and I wonder if my life would have been different if he'd been there for us.

I have trouble accepting his death because there's no body, no burial place. There was never a ceremony. He just came to California and disappeared. I know it's stupid, but when I go by a church on Sunday, listening to the voices, I always pause to hear the preacher's voice because... I'm not sure why since I wouldn't know Pa's voice if I heard it.

I listen to the choir sing "In the sweet by and by." Maybe we'll get to meet then.

I listen to the choir sing "Abide with me," but I'm not

good at abiding.

I've tried to gather all the facts I can about Pa. I know
he was a ministerial student at Georgetown College when
you met him, and I know he took over the pastorate at the
New Hope Baptist Church when the two of you came to
Clay County. I know he was one of the men who helped to
found William Jewell College in Liberty and that he was on
the board of trustees. And I know he left for California a
year after the gold rush and that you heard from him for the
last time when he was near Marysville.

I know he told you "to kiss Jesse for me and tell
Franklin to be a good boy and learn fast." He said "Pray for
me that if no more we meet in this world we can meet in
Glory."

But all I have are those words written in fading ink and
they're not enough. That's why I'm here.

The land is arid, the temperature's often over a hundred,
but there are oak and olive trees, and in the winter they say
you can see the snow on the Sierras. Right now, that's hard
to believe.

I've talked to a lot of men I've met in this area. I always
have the same conversation.

"Do you remember a Baptist minister named Robert
James? He came here shortly after the gold rush."

Sometimes they'll ask me what he looks like and I'm
not sure what to tell them. I seem to remember clinging to
his leg and crying, "Please, Daddy, don't go. I don't want
you to go," but maybe you just told me that story. Or maybe
it's something I've imagined.

Later, I know I used to cry myself to sleep when you
were married to Mr. Simms. I'd bang my head against the
pillow, not accepting my fate (I've never been good at accepting what I don't like) and cry, "I want my Pa to come
back." But he never did, not even in my dreams. Sometimes
I'll see his hands or his boots but his face has always been
blurred.

I wanted to have lots of pictures taken when I was

younger.

I ask everyone I meet. "Did you know a minister named Robert James?" I've asked men working their claims and I've asked in bars and restaurants. I must have said it ten thousand times. "Did you know a minister named Robert James?" I've asked it so often that I find myself walking away before they have a chance to answer. I already know what they'll say.

Probably it seems morbid for someone as young as me to be obsessed with dying, but I've come close so many times I think I know more about death than most men. When I die, I want to have a proper service and burial so people will be able to know I was here. They'll be able to visit my resting place and, if they want to, put a flower on my grave.

I want people to be able to say, "Jesse James was here."

> Love,
> Jesse

St. Helena, California
July 16, 1868

Dear Zee,

The Napa Valley is beautiful.

For as far as you can see, there are vineyards and, right now, the grapes are being harvested. Everywhere I go, I see men stooped over the vines, picking the purple grapes, and when you go by the stone wineries you see people crushing the grapes and yelling to one another in the drunken air.

You see couples sitting at redwood tables under the large oaks in the valley. They'll have picnic lunches and a bottle or two of wine and they'll touch each other, not really seeing the vineyards or the old oaks covered with mistletoe or the nearby mill, just seeing each other, and it makes me hurt inside because I miss you.

I remember how you stood beneath the mistletoe that

first Christmas and said, "Kiss me," and I thought you were forward. But I kissed you anyway. And asked if I could kiss you again.

It never seems to rain in the summer. The days are warm, sunny, but the nights are cool and there's no humidity. The people don't have to sleep out on their porches the way they do in Missouri, But I miss the green hills (it's drier here) and the lightning in the mountains.

I went to see a geyser—the water shoots up from the ground about every hour—up the valley, and I walked along a creek, barefoot, stepping from stone to stone, looking at the pollywogs flit back and forth in the glassy water.

I visited a small waterfall in the mountains where the trees leaned out over the stream. The leaves were long and lance shaped and when you crumpled them between your fingers, they smelled sweet. Pungent. Some of the people here put the leaves into spaghetti.

George and Becky Turner took me to the Sonoma Valley, west of here, and we visited the Sonoma Mission, which was the last one built by the padres as they came north and I imagined them making the long ride on mules, sweating in their dark cassocks. Then we visited an adobe fort that was built by General Vallejo near Petaluma and there was a celebration going on. They were all laughing and dancing and drinking, all sure they'd never die, and I felt that old ache come back there beneath the orange moon.

I'm not sure of anything, but I remember dancing outdoors with you beneath the colored lanterns hanging from the trees and it's summer, and I remember the sound of the fiddles and the fiddler yelling, "Change partners," but I pretend not to hear him. I want to keep dancing with you. I know I'm not much of a dancer, but I almost get dizzy, circling the floor with you, holding you as close as I possibly can. I say, "I may be one of the most wanted men in America, but I don't care about that. I'm just glad you want me. That's all that matters."

You say, "I'll always want you," and you pull me so

close the people around us stare; but I don't care.

I was asked, "What do you miss most about Missouri?" and I knew immediately, although I didn't answer the question. It's the feel of you... the feel of you... the feel of you.

Jesse

somewhere in the midwest
October 10, 1868

Dear Susan,

It's a long ride home. Monotonous. At first I enjoyed looking at the trees turning color, but after awhile one tree looks like another and the prairie never seems to change.

People on the train play cards or read or talk, but after awhile they run out of things to say and the card games and the books become dull. After awhile the best thing you can do is sleep, but the seats are uncomfortable and the train clatters across the rails and the smoke and soot from the engine drift back to the passenger section, burning your eyes, and sleep is impossible.

The Reno Brothers held up the first train ever robbed in this country two years ago this month. Now I know why. They must have taken a long train ride and they wanted to get even with the railroad.

It could give a man ideas.

This morning the train had to slow down for a huge herd of buffalo. There were so many of them that, at a distance, it looked as if the whole prairie had broken out in cankers. When the herd got closer, you could see flies buzzing around them and it was like something I dreamt once. A kind of nightmare that crushed my chest and I woke up breathing hard.

Men on the train grabbed their rifles and began shooting the beasts. I think they killed them because it gave them something to do. It alleviated the boredom. Sometimes I think it doesn't take much to make a man a killer.

It takes a heavy caliber bullet to stop a buffalo but most of the men had Sharps; I hadn't smelled so much gunpowder since the war. It was like someone was burning cordite in the car. My eyes became even more inflamed than they were. The firing of the guns and the grunting sound the beasts made when they were shot blended with the train's whistle and the sound of the wheels on the tracks. Death death death death death. It was palpable. You could hear it.

When some of the bulls were wounded, they'd charge the train and a few of them actually managed to butt the train. You could feel it shake but the bulls must have broken their skulls on the iron and it was terrible to watch them quiver and go down.

A lot of them snorted when they were shot. You could see the blood spurt out their nostrils, then they'd snort again, choking and dying on their own blood, their eyes wild and strange.

The men shooting them would fire as fast as they could and most of them talked to themselves between shots. They said things like. "Got you, you bastard. Die. DIE." Sometimes you'd hear the buffaloes' legs crack when they collapsed and it was like listening to someone snap a stick on a cold day.

Finally, I turned away but the rhythm of the carnage was in my blood. Death death death death death. The sound of it came up into my ears, chuffing and terrible, like a boiler ready to explode.

Jesse

Kearney
October 21, 1868

Dear Belle

Ma began yelling almost as soon as I got in the door. "Do you know that Nimrod Long, the man you shot in Russellville, gave your Pa the money he needed to attend

Georgetown College so he could become a preacher?"

"I didn't shoot Long."

"I don't care who shot him. You were there."

"How was I supposed to know he gave Pa money? He was just some guy who got in the way. If he'd been smart, he wouldn't have run."

"Is that the thanks we give people—shooting them—for helping out the family? *Is it?*"

Zee had come to the farm to welcome me home. She and Ma had cooked a pork roast and potatoes and they'd made a large salad, but Ma began to shout before we sat down.

"When I'm not explaining your actions to the Pinkertons and to the law, I'm busy praying for you," Ma yelled.

"I've never asked you to explain anything to anyone."

"Someone's always coming around here. Snooping."

"Never asked you to pray."

"I'm down on my hands and knees, praying, 'Oh Lord, save my son Jesse,' when I'm not scrubbing floors."

"Ma, stop it," Zee cried.

"I may be related to you, but I'm not your Ma... yet." She continued, "I tell the newspaper people, 'I'm proud of my children. I'm proud to be the mother of Frank and Jesse James. They've never wronged anyone,' then you make a liar out of me."

"Ma, I didn't come home to argue," I said.

"I tell the reporters, 'They're good boys.' I tell them —"

"SHIT."

"Don't use that language in this house."

"I never should have come home," I yelled and ran out the door.

"Wait," said Zee, coming after me, but I walked as fast as I could until I was a hundred yards or so from the house.

When Zee reached me, she didn't say anything at first. She just stood there staring, then we leaned against a tree, catching our breath. The leaves were turning red and yellow.

Zee said, "I never meant to pry into your affairs. To

nag you. I just want to be a good wife for you... someday."

At first I didn't know what she was talking about, then I remembered what I'd written her from Texas. She was always asking questions: What did I do? Why was I gone so long? Where was I? Why did I have so many guns?

"I don't mean to be like your Ma," Zee said. "I don't mean to hound you."

"Zee, I try to be as good a man as I can," I said. I felt tired. "I know you and Ma both mean well. Both love me. But I can't be someone I'm not. You have to remember that."

"I know."

I let my head rest against the trunk of the tree. I could feel the bark against my neck. Feel the wool collar of my shirt... rubbing.

"Zee, I'm only twenty-one, but I already feel old. Sometimes I can barely hold my head up."

Then I almost slid to the ground, like someone drunk, the bark scraping my neck, and I sat there stupidly on the dank earth. The red and yellow leaves blew into my face, but I didn't even blink.

Zee bent over me, saying, "Are you all right, are you all right?" but I didn't answer her.

I remembered the time you were angry with your mother and father and you said, "It's too bad we have to be born into this world with parents."

I told you, "You shouldn't say that. It's against the Commandments. 'Honor thy mother and father.'"

"Oh, bullshit, Jesse. God never had my folks for parents."

Sometimes I know what you mean.

Jesse

1869-1874

Kearney
November 7, 1869

Dear Cole,

Since the war, I'll wake up in the middle of the night, suffocating.

In the dream I'm having, a blue belly with no face is stuffing my head into a sack and tying a noose around my neck. I'm on a horse and my legs grip his sides so hard I feel my muscles ache. I can feel the sweat roll down the sides of my face. I can't see anything but my hearing has never been more acute.

I'm waiting (w-a-i-t-i-n-g) for someone to shout or for a whip to cut through the air, hitting the horse.

It takes a long time.

"We'll be rid of another one in a minute," the blue belly says, then I hear the whip moving through the air, hear it crack against the haunches of my horse. Just before I'm lifted off the saddle, dangling in the air, I sit up, gasping for breath.

I don't know if I take morphine to numb my war wounds or to numb the way I feel. Maybe both.

One day has just faded into the next for a year now. I know most people spend their lives like this, dulling the way they feel a little more each day, until dying is becoming. It seems insane to me.

I've helped build a mill and swapped cattle at livestock shows. I've plowed fields and told myself, it's an honorable profession, that it goes back to Biblical days, but I'm bored. Restless. At noon I'm taking morphine to help me get through the day and by the middle of the afternoon I'm moving in slow motion.

I tried selling coal, but I'll never be a salesman.

My first day at work I visited more than two dozen farms, always asking the same question, "Do you need any coal?" and each time the person I talked to said, "No," shutting the door in my face. By the end of the afternoon I wanted to kill someone.

When I talked to my boss that night he said, "Damn it, Jesse, don't you know how to do anything?"

I almost pulled a gun on him. Then I would have shown the bastard what I can do.

He said, "People expect you to be friendly, to smile." Then he smiled like an idiot. I wanted to knock that grin off his face, but I just stood there, clenching my hands. Tight. My eyes shut.

"What's the matter?" he asked. "Are you afraid to look me in the eye? Maybe that's what's wrong? You're afraid to look at people. Is that it?"

I kept telling myself: I don't have to take this, I don't have to take this. "Just shut up," I mumbled.

I don't think he heard me. He said, "People expect you to come to their door with some funny stories, to amuse them. You can't just knock on their door and stick a lump of coal in their face."

"Just shut up," I said again. A little louder this time.

"What did you say?"

"You heard me."

"Say it to my face," he yelled.

"If you yell at me again, *I'll kill you*," I said. I was breathing faster and I tried to tell myself: Just take it easy. Easy. You don't want to kill anyone. Not now. Not like this. I took some deep breaths and blinked to bring things back into focus.

"Get out of here."

"Glad to," I said, walking out the door—the freest man alive.

When I got home Ma asked, "How was your day?" but I didn't answer her until I'd mixed some morphine and water and drunk it.

"I don't think it went too well," I finally said. Then I went out onto the porch and sat down.

It had been worse than the worst day we ever had in the war, Cole. People shouldn't let themselves be mistreated or belittled. They ought to fight back. We didn't let the Yanks walk over us, and I'm not ready to have some piss-ant merchant insult me now.

Let's rob another bank. Soon.

Jesse

Kearney
December 14, 1869

Dear Cole,

Frank recognized him as soon as we walked into the Daviess County Savings Bank in Gallatin.

"Who said there isn't a Santa Claus?" Frank asked.

I went over the cashier's window and said, "Bill Anderson sends his regards."

Captain Sheets looked up from his desk and said, "Bill Anderson's been dead six years."

"I know. You helped to kill him. You and Major Cox. I was there that day, too."

Frank and I pulled our pistols. I pointed mine at Sheets and Frank covered his assistant. I said, "You didn't even have the decency to face Bill and his men. You had to ambush them."

I remembered all of the things Bill did for me. He let me ride with him when no one else would. He gave me a chance. Someone told me he'd said, "Not to have any beard, Jesse is the keenest and cleanest fighter in the command." I'll never forget that. He didn't believe in shooting people in the back. The man had courage, and he instilled it in those who followed him.

Sheets said, "It was the war. You have to understand."

"Yeah, probably it was all Cox's fault."

"Yes."

"You're really a great guy."

He was starting to look hopeful.

"Practically a saint."

"Well, I wouldn't say that."

"Maybe it was an accident."

"Maybe so," Sheets said.

"Maybe a big misunderstanding."

"Yes."

"Your gun was pointed at Bill and it just happened to go off."

Sheets nodded, smiling, as I pulled the trigger.

"Accidents happen," I said.

> Merry Christmas,
> Jesse

Harlem
January 2, 1870

Dear Cole,

Frank and I were in the stable when the little darkie who helps Ma out around the house came running toward us in the twilight. All you could see was his silhouette and his white teeth.

When he came into the stable, he said, "Massa Frank, Massa Jesse, there's some strange men out dere. Two of dem are comin' up the path toward the house an' anudder two are hidin' in the woods out back. Missus Samuel said to tell you."

Frank looked around the door. "I can see the two coming toward the house, Jesse."

There was half an inch of snow on the ground and the wind whipped it around the men. It looked like they were stepping out of a cyclone made of snow.

"Damn it, they must have figured out that was my horse we left behind in Gallatin," I said.

"There's no way they could be sure."

"Apparently, they don't care about being sure. They just care about getting even. For some reason Sheets was a popular man there."

"Damned if I know why. He didn't seem to have much

personality to me."

"Me neither."

When Frank and I were leaving the bank, my horse had been spooked by the shot I'd fired. When I tried to mount him, he kept bucking and snorting and I was half-dragged down the street with one foot in the stirrup before I finally managed to get loose. Then I jumped up behind Frank. "I never did like that horse," I said.

"We won't get very far riding double," Frank said. "Right about now I can understand why Richard the Third said he'd give his kingdom for a horse."

"What a time to be thinking of Shakespeare," I said.

Frank and I told the darkie to go back to the house as we mounted up. We hunched over our horses, opening the stable doors just enough to get through. We kept our hands on our horses' mouths to keep them from neighing, but we could see their breath in the air.

As the darkie reached our porch, Frank and I spurred our horses. They jumped the fence around the barn-lot as the men near the house began firing at us and the two riders came down out of the trees.

One of the men dismounted and took a shot as us with his rifle. When he did, his horse must've broken loose because it caught up to us before we'd gone half a mile.

Frank pulled his pistol and leaned toward the horse running beside him. His gun was almost touching the horse's head when he pulled the trigger. BLAM. The horse kind of somersaulted to a stop in the snow. Except for the blood, it looked like someone had sprinkled it with sugar.

"Sure is a sight," Frank said. "The posse man who owns that horse will have sore feet and a cold butt by the time he gets home tonight."

"Yeah, I'll bet he'd trade his kingdom, if he had one, for another horse," I said.

Happy New Year,
Jesse

Southern Iowa
Saturday, June 3, 1871

Dear Susan,

We rode into Corydon, pretending to be cattle buyers. We wore linen dusters so we could hide the grain sacks.

It was humid, and the heat seemed to come up at us through the soles of our boots.

Frank and Jim held the horses while Cole and I went into the bank.

Cole handed the cashier a hundred dollar bill and said, "Could you change this for me?"

"I'm afraid I can't, sir. The treasurer of the bank has the only key to the safe, and he's taking part in a debate at the edge of town."

"What's the debate about?" I asked.

"We're trying to decide where to build the new school house. Some people think it should be in one place and others think it ought to be somewhere else. I don't know that it makes any real difference, as long as we get it, but you couldn't tell that to the folks out there."

Cole said, "I wish we could listen to them for awhile. It might be good for a few laughs. But we haven't got the time. Where do you think we can get this bill cashed?"

"Maybe at the Ocobock Brothers' Bank across the street. It's a new one in town. I hope they can help you."

I smiled. "I hope so too."

"It's devoutly to be wished," Cole said. It was something he'd heard Frank say when he was reading Shakespeare. For awhile Cole would say, "It's devoutly to be wished" when he was going to the store to buy cigars. He'd wink at Frank. "Don't you think so?"

We crossed the street, waving to Frank and Jim so they'd know everything was all right. We could hear the debaters' voices at the edge of town, but there wasn't any other sound except for the neighing of one of the horses and Cole's spurs jangling.

Inside the bank, the heat was almost explosive. You had

the feeling the air would blow up if you lit a match. Cole handed the clerk the hundred and asked, "Can you cash this for me?"

"Certainly, sir." He was a pleasant little fellow. He went to the vault and when he came back with the money we had our guns out.

"I think we'll need a little more money than we planned on," I said. "Get back to the vault."

We tied the clerk up, then filled the grain sacks with all the bills we could find. We were about to leave when an old darkie came in. He was a preacher and he wanted to make a deposit. He said, "Praise the Lord, I had a great bunch of sinners in my congregation."

"Well, the Lord always says it's better to give than to receive," Cole said, "so I'd hand the money over unless you want to get to heaven faster than you planned." Cole stuck his pistol in the preacher's face.

"No, sir, I ain't in that much of a hurry to get there."

"I'm glad to hear that, reverend." Cole took the money and we tied the darkie up next to the cashier. Both of them were gagged.

I told Cole, "It's so hot I'll bet their teeth are sweating."

When we were leaving I tipped my hat to the men we'd tied up and said, "Praise the Lord. He certainly does work in mysterious ways."

"He does indeed," Cole said, laughing, and we went back out onto the street.

We mounted our horses and rode past the debaters at the edge of town. "Hold on a second," I told the boys, "let's listen to them."

An orator named Henry Clay Dean was busy damning everything his opponent had said. Maybe because of the heat, he sounded like he was trying to gargle and speak at the same time. The words kind of gurgled out of him.

"Excuse me," I yelled.

He paused, looking over our way. "What is it?"

"May I ask a question?"

"If it's important enough to interrupt this discussion, which it obviously is, I'll yield to you. What's your question? "

He was the kind of person who had to use nineteen words when one would do. Apparently, the only word he didn't know how to say was yes.

"I think there's something wrong down at the Ocobock Brothers' Bank."

"What makes you think that?"

"Well, the boys and I were just there and we took all of the cash we could find with us. When we left, the clerk and some old darkie who was sputtering about the Lord were trying to carry on a conversation but they were having a hard time because they were both chewing on cotton. Someone ought to go down there and take the gags our of their mouths. "

"Are you saying—"

"Jesse James was here," I said and fired a shot into the air. Then Jim, Cole and Frank fired their revolvers and everyone in the crowd ducked. I think they were sure the notorious James Gang was going to murder them all. You know what lies some of the papers have printed about us.

I'm wanted for some things I did, but I'm wanted for a lot more I didn't do. So, what the hell. I might as well put my signature on history. Might as well let the world know who I am, even if I'm not always sure myself.

Jesse

Kansas City, Missouri
September 29, 1872

Dear Belle,

Frank, Cole and I got away with $978 three days ago when we seized the cash box at the Kansas City Fair. If we'd been there a few minutes earlier, we'd have walked off with thou-sands. Someone had just taken the day's receipts to the bank.

But it was exciting, the three of us riding into the fair-grounds in front of ten thousand people. We waved at everyone and smiled. I think they thought we were going to put on a show of some kind. At least we provided a little action, gave them something to write home about.

"Hell, I feel like I ought to stop and sign autographs," Cole said.

"Let's take care of business first."

I strolled over to the cashier and said, "What if I told you I'm Jesse James and that you'd better give me that cash box if you want to see what tomorrow looks like?"

"I'd tell you to go to hell," he said.

"Well, that's who I am, Jesse James. You may not know this, but I'm a better magician than the one who's appearing here. All I have to do is take this Colt out, aim it at you and pull the trigger and, mister, you'll do the biggest disappearing act ever invented." I leveled my pistol at him. "Now. Do you want to disappear?"

He decided he didn't want to be part of the magic act. When he handed over the money, Cole, Frank and I were the ones who disappeared.

Today there was an editorial titled "The Chivalry of Crime" by Major John Newman Edwards in the Kansas City *Times*. He says the way we live is "poetic, superb."

"Listen to this," I told Cole. "'There are men in Jackson, Cass and Clay Counties who learned to dare when there was no such word as quarter in the dictionary of the Border. Men who have carried their lives in their hands so long that they do not know how to commit them over into the keeping of the laws and regulations that exist now, and these men sometimes rob. But it is always in the glare of day and in the teeth of the multitude. With them booty is but the second thought; the wild drama of the adventure first. These men never go upon the highway in lonesome places to plunder the pilgrim. That they leave to the ignoble pack of jackals. But they ride at midday into the county seat, while court is sitting, take the cash out of the vault and put the cashier in and ride out of town to the music of cracking pistols.'"

"Don't that man have a way with words?" Cole said.

I continued. "'These men are bad citizens but they are bad because they live out of their time. The nineteenth century with its Sybaric civilization is not the social soil for men who might have sat with Arthur at the Round Table, ridden tourney with Sir Lancelot or won the colors of Guinevere; men who might have shattered the casque of Brian de Bois Guilbert, shivered a lance with Ivanhoe or won the smile of a Hebrew maiden; the men who could have met Turpin and Duval and robbed them of their ill-gotten booty on Hounslow Heath.'"

"Damn if it isn't good to know we went bad because of the 'Sybaric civilization' we're part of. All this time I thought it was because I'm an asshole."

"'Such as these are they who awed the multitude on Thursday. What they did we condemn. But the way they did it we cannot help admiring. It was as though three bandits had come to us from the storied Odenwald, with the halo of medieval chivalry upon their garments and shown us how things were done that poets sing of.'"

"I met a poet once," Cole interrupted. "It was during the war. He was always asking you questions about life and he went around calling everyone his brother. The tree was his brother, the whore his brother (figure that one out), the men who were going into battle. All brothers. He was a weird son-of-a-bitch. A poet. I never understood a fuckin' thing he said."

"'Nowhere else in the United States or in the civilized world, probably, could this thing have been done. It was done here, not because the protectors of person and property were less efficient but because the bandits were more dashing and skillful; not because honest Missourians have less nerve but because free-booting Missourians have more.'"

"I like that man," Cole said. "He understands us."

"Yeah, someday we'll have to meet him."

Meanwhile, Cole sends his love.

Jesse

Hermann, Missouri
June 30, 1873

Dear Belle,

Downstairs, I can hear a piano playing and, once in awhile, someone's laughter. Maybe it's Cole's.

When we robbed the St. Genevieve bank earlier this month, a posse trailed us out of town but, like most posses, they didn't want to get *too* close to us.

We got away with almost $4,000 and it was one of those days that's so beautiful you know you're never going to die. I don't feel like that very often.

I'd composed some short notes on scraps of paper. They were like the sayings the Chinese put in fortune cookies but instead of giving your fortune they said, "Married men turn around and go home. Single men follow." And "We'll be in Kansas City on the 29th, and in Hermann on the 30th. Come and see us."

I laughed, my face lifted to the sun, as I scattered the notes behind us on the trail.

Frank said, "That must be the stupidest thing you've ever done," but he has as much humor as a rock.

Cole was laughing. "Hell, it don't make no difference. None of us plan to be there."

I said, "That's what the law will think. Let's surprise them."

"*You* surprise them," Frank said. "You're asking to be killed."

Zee told me the same thing, but she's supposed to say that. Supposed to watch out for me since we're going to be married. If it were up to her, I'd still be pushing a plow and the worst thing I'd have to worry about was being kicked by a mule. She kept saying, "Don't do it, Jesse. It's crazy. Don't go."

"It'll be fun," I said. "It'll show I haven't lost my nerve."

"No one's ever accused you of that."

"Well, I don't want them to."

Later on, I asked Cole if he thought I was crazy and he told me, "You're the craziest son-of-a-bitch I know, but I want to go with you. I can use some laughs."

When we arrived in Hermann earlier today, checking into the hotel, Cole told the desk clerk, "This is a mighty nice looking town. Mighty nice. Yes, sir."

"We like it here," the clerk said. He was a skinny guy with pimples and he had a scared look about him. You knew he'd never leave the place. Never travel more than ten miles away because he wouldn't know what to expect. He has to convince himself it's great here or go crazy. You could almost smell his fear when he asked where we were from and I said, "Kansas City."

"That's a pretty big town, isn't it?"

"Yeah," Cole said, "I heard about a guy who came there the other day from the country. It was so big he must have got confused somehow. No one ever saw him again." Cole shook his head and tried to look as sorrowful as possible. "It was tragic. Tragic."

"No one gets lost here."

I said, "We thought about settling down in a safe place like this, but we heard there was a bank robbery here a week ago. I guess a man isn't safe anyplace these days."

The clerk nodded, looking more worried than before.

"Well, I wouldn't worry about it," Cole laughed. "They say lightning never strikes twice in the same place."

When we went to dinner Cole told the waiter he wanted "the biggest, bloodiest steak you've got in this place," and he thumped the table. "Be sure to tell the chef I want it rare, understand?"

I said, "If he could, he'd go up to a steer on the prairie and hit it on the head with a hammer, then cut a chunk out of it and devour it raw. I saw him do it once."

The waiter looked at Cole as if he believed it.

For a moment I thought Cole was going to order chili. The last time he did he almost shouted his order, saying, "I like it HOT, the way I like my women," then he slapped his knee and began to laugh. "Har har har." You know that big laugh he has. It rumbles up from his belly and erupts. Sometimes he embarrasses Frank.

Cole was really wound up by the time we went into the saloon after dinner. He said, "I want to buy everyone here a drink and listen to what you have to say about the robbery the other day."

Everyone at the bar said it was about the scariest thing that had ever happened in Hermann. Several of them told us they'd hidden behind the bar until the bank robbers had left town.

Cole told them he'd fought for the Confederacy. "I was willing to give my life for my ideals," he said, holding his hat over his heart and looking solemn. "I've stared Death in the face many times and never shrunk from it."

"Ah, bullshit," someone said. "You'd have been hiding behind the bar, too."

"The hell I would," Cole roared. "I would have run to the door and let those robbers have it. I'd have gone out into the street and faced them down, a gun in each hand. Blazing away. I'd have shot them so full of holes they'd look like a Swiss cheese."

"BULLSHIT!"

Neither Cole nor I were wearing our guns but he pretended to draw, pointing both fingers at the people around him. "I'd have showed those bandits," he said. "I'd have blown their asses off," and he imitated the sound a gun makes.

He was so entranced with his own story that he didn't even know it when I left the bar.

I can hear him all the way up here. "BLAM BLAM BLAM BLAM BLAM."

Those outlaws must be mighty dead by now.

Jesse

Des Moines, Iowa
July 22, 1873.

Dear Belle,

Last night we tried robbing a train.

Well, why not? We've tried banks and stage coaches, and the tip we received said this train was supposed to be loaded with Yankee dollars on their way to Chicago.

Sometimes I think we'll end up robbing cigar stores or creeping into wigwams and stealing from the Indians. Sometimes I'd like to get out of the business, but I'm trapped now. Even when I began, I never felt I had any choice.

I was a kid when they shot me down and all I'd done was ride with Quantrill and Anderson because I was too young for the regular army.

Sometimes I feel sick.

When we arrived in Adair, we went to the depot. Everything was closed down and the town was darker than the inside of a darky's coat pocket.

We waited out a ways from the depot, then pulled some spikes from the tracks. I thought someone would hear us because of the noise the hammer made hitting steel, but the people in Adair must have good hearts and the ability to sleep through anything. I wish I did. More and more, I get up in the middle of the night, walking around the house, listening to every board creak, waiting for dawn.

We tied ropes to the track and had our horses pull the rails out of alignment, figuring the train would stop when it got there.

We waited and waited in the dark, whispering like fools. "Do you think we got a bad tip?"

"Hell, I don't know. But I'm tired of standing here."

"Yeah, time sure passes when you're having fun."

Then, suddenly, we could hear the train. It came chugging toward us about midnight and when it came to the curve where we'd pulled the rails apart, its wheels jumped the track and the train toppled over on its side like some beast going down in the jungle. You could hear the metal twist, and I thought the boiler was going to explode. Inside, the passengers were screaming.

"What the hell have we done?" Frank asked.

"Damned if I know," Cole answered, "but we may as well go after the money."

We went to the express car and the guard opened the safe without arguing, but there was only three thousand dollars inside.

Cole said, "Tell us where you've hidden the rest of the money."

"There isn't any hidden money. This is it. Just don't kill me. I've done my best to cooperate."

"Oh, the hell with him," I said.

We went back to the daycoach, figuring we could get some money from the passengers, but the coach was filled with about thirty Chinamen. "Where the hell did they find so many Chinks?" Cole asked.

"Maybe they work for the railroad," Frank said.

They were screaming, but it sounded as if they were trying to sing off-key.

· Cole fired a shot in the air to get their attention.

They stopped screaming for a few seconds and he went up to one of them. They were all wearing silk pajamas and funny hats that were shaped like mushrooms. Cole stuck his gun in the stomach of one of the men and said, "Listen, give me your money or I'm going to shoot you. When the bullet comes out your backside you're going to think you have two assholes, one for weekdays and one for Sundays. Understand?"

The Chinaman looked confused. "Ash holes?" he asked.

Assholes," Cole said. "What you shit with. But you'll have two of them."

The Chinaman Cole was talking to said something to the one next to him and they both began singing, at least it sounded like singing.

"What the hell are you talking about?" Cole yelled.

"They don't understand you," Frank said.

"Why the hell not? I'm speaking perfectly good English, ain't I?"

Frank grabbed a grain sack and held it in front of the Chinaman who was doing most of the singing. "Here," he said, "put all your valuables in here."

The Chinaman looked at Frank, looked at Cole, and then stuck his head into the sack like it was a grab-bag or something and we were all playing a game. You could still hear him singing with his head covered up.

"You stupid son-of-a-bitch," Cole yelled, "get your yellow head out of there!" He put the barrel of his pistol into the Chinaman's butt and for a second I really thought he was going to end up with two assholes.

"Let me try to communicate with them again," Frank said. He pretended to empty his pockets, saying, "That ought to give them the idea."

Cole said, "The heathen bastards don't have no pockets. Can't you see that?"

"Yeah. Well—" All the Shakespeare in the world hadn't prepared Frank for that. You know how he prides himself on being such a great communicator.

None of us knew what to do.

Finally, Cole said, "To paraphrase the immortal bard in *Julius Caesar*, 'The hell with the dumb fucks,'" and we got out of the car and mounted our horses.

The engine was still hissing and the Chinese were more excited than ever and we were cold and tired and a long way from home.

I said, "Remind me never to go to China."

Jesse

Kearney
August 15, 1873

Dear Belle,

Detectives from the Pinkerton Agency in Chicago have

come into the area, looking for Frank and me, but everyone
they talk to in Clay County gives them a different description. The people around here know we're not bad.

We aren't telling the widowed or maimed or bankrupt
to put the few possessions they've spent a lifetime accumu-
lating into their broken-down wagons, pushing them off their
land.

I was riding near Excelsior Springs yesterday when a
Pinkerton man approached me. He didn't tell me he was a
Pinkerton man but you can always tell. Coming from Chicago, they don't sound the way our people do. And most of
them wear suits and derby hats. They think they're fooling
people, pretending to be everything but what they are, but
they might as well hang a big sign around their necks:
PINKERTON MAN.

"Nice country around here," the Pinkerton man said.

"Yes, it is."

"I've been thinking about buying a farm in the area."

"Lots of them for sale 'cause of the banks."

"That's what I've heard," the Pinkerton man said. "I'm
particularly interested in buying something over near Kearney."

"I think I'd stay away from there," I said. "I hear Jesse
James is from that area."

"So I've heard. I guess he can be pretty dangerous."

"Absolutely ruthless, I've been told," I said. "A mean,
heathen bastard."

"A man without conscience."

"An animal."

"I guess the whole bunch in that area is pretty desperate," the Pinkerton man said: "Frank James, the Youngers."

"Stealing, lying, fornicating, I hear they've invented
sins that aren't even listed in the Commandments."

"Maybe you can tell me where to find them," the Pinkerton man said.

""Well, I'll tell you just so you won't get too close to
them," I said. "The last I heard Jesse was pretending to be
in the coal business. Had a little place over near Kearney."

68

"What's he look like? Just so I'll be sure to avoid him if I ever happen to cross his path."

"He's just over six feet tall, has dark hair, and he looks like he's in his mid-thirties. Can't be that old, of course, but a life of crime has prematurely aged him."

"You wonder what turns some men bad," the Pinkerton man said.

"Maybe they're just born rotten."

"Well, I'm glad there's one good person around here who doesn't think Jesse James is Robin Hood."

"No, you'd never catch Jesse wearing green," I said.

He looked baffled when I told him that, then he said, "Oh, now I get it. Robin Hood. Green." And he began to laugh.

He was still laughing when he rode off, but not as hard as I was.

Jesse

Kearney
February 5, 1874

Dear Belle,

If at first you don't succeed, try, try again a teacher of mine said. Thinking back on it, he was a doddering old fool.

We robbed another train.

Around five-thirty in the afternoon, five of us went into the depot at Gads Hill, pointing our guns at the station agent and a few men who were spitting tobacco and talking about the weather. I've seen hound dogs too lazy to scratch fleas that were more energetic than the folk lounging around there. I think they spend their time betting on slug races.

"Is this really a stick-up?" one of them asked.

Cole said, "We ain't here to play Chinese checkers."

"No, we should have brought them along when we stuck up the train at Adair," I said.

"There's a kill-joy in every bunch," Cole replied.

We had the station agent put out a signal flag on the tracks so the train would stop there. It was going to be headed south to Little Rock.

When the train stopped, I went up to the conductor and said, "When you see the reporters, tell them you talked to Jesse James."

Cole and his brothers got the contents of the safe from the express car while Frank and I went through the passenger coach. We looked at the hands of each man there.

Frank said, "We don't want to rob workingmen or ladies; we just want the money and valuables of the plug-hat gentlemen."

We thought one of the passengers was a Pinkerton man and said, "We'd like to talk to you—privately."

By that time the rest of the boys had come onto the coach.

Cole and I took the guy to one of the private compartments. Cole pointed his pistol at him and said, "If it goes off now and you survive, you're going to be talking in a falsetto for the rest of your life. Take your clothes off and be quick about it unless you want to sing opera."

"Why?"

"Just do it."

Cole even made him get out of his longjohns. His knees were clinking so badly from the cold that he could have been sending Morse code.

We looked through all his pockets for any signs that he might be a Pinkerton man, but we didn't find anything. No identification. No gun. Nothing.

Just before we left Cole told the guy, "You'd better hurry up and get them clothes back on before it shrivels up and disappears completely. Course there ain't much there to begin with."

The man shivered, trying to cover himself with his hands, his eyes as large as those of a doe in the dark. When Cole slammed the door, it made me realize how alone we all are. And I felt sorry for the man, but I didn't tell Cole that.

Before we left the station I gave the agent a press release and said, "Give this to the newspaper. We like to do things in style." It was headed "The Most Daring Train Robbery on Record!" and ended with "There is a hell of an excitement in this part of the country."

If you don't pat yourself on the back, who will?

But when we counted the money, all we had to show for our work was two thousand dollars.

"Hell," Cole said. "The governor of Missouri is offering that much for the 'bodies of each of the robbers,' according to the newspapers. We're worth more dead than we are alive."

"If he expects me to throw myself down in front of the next train I see in order to increase my net worth, he's crazy," I said. "But listen to Major John Newman Edwards' editorial. He claims we're 'strong, hardy men—men who risk much, who have friends in high places, and who go riding over the land, taking all chances that come in the way, and spending lavishly tomorrow what is won today at the muzzle of a revolver.'"

"You know, I like that man more and more."

Jesse

February 6, 1874

Dear Major Edwards,

I can't tell you where I am, not now, probably not ever, but I want you to know I appreciate much that you've written about us.

After we were in Gads Hill, Frank and I separated from the men who were with us, and we headed home through the Iron Mountains. They're as bleak and hard as their name indicates, particularly during the winter.

We stopped at a small cabin around noon. A woman in her late twenties came out onto the porch when we reined up there. Her hair was dark, tied in a bun, and her clothes were

worn from too many washings. The fabric had faded so
badly it was difficult to tell what color it had been.

Frank took his hat off and said, "We'd appreciate it if
you could feed us lunch, ma'am. We'll be glad to pay you."

"I don't have much, just some cheese and apples, and
some chili that's in the pot, but you're welcome to that."

We went into the house and the woman told us her
name was Mrs. Settle. Her husband had fought in the Confederacy and he never came marching home. She said, "I'm
not even sure where he was buried," and she began to cry.
"They ought to have left me with that much, at least there
ought to be a grave I can lay flowers on, but here I am feeling sorry for myself again. It doesn't help."

When we had eaten, I gave her ten dollars and she began
to sob. Her whole body shook.

I said, "Ma'am, if you don't feel like we've paid you
enough, we'd be glad to give you more."

"No, it's not that. You've been more than generous,"
she said. "I know this place doesn't look like much and it
doesn't offer me much in the way of a living, but it's all I've
got and this afternoon I won't even have that anymore."

"Why not?" Frank asked.

"I owe the bank five hundred dollars and the manager's
coming to foreclose on the property this afternoon. In a few
hours, the only thing I'll own will be a few pots and pans
and the clothes on my back."

We were standing on the porch when she told us that.
At first, neither Frank nor I knew what to do so we walked
down the stairs and mounted our horses, looking at each
other. Then we both nodded at the same time and Frank
said, "We'll give you the money."

I don't think she heard him at first. Or maybe she didn't
believe what she'd heard. There was a kind of whoosh when
she let out what must have been a long breath and she said,
"Why would you do that?"

We didn't know ourselves. It just pained us to see a
decent, generous woman lose everything to some banker

who'd probably never worked a day in his life and we told her so. When we gave her the money Frank said, "Just be sure you recover the note when you pay the banker."

"Yes, of course," she said, then she told us a lot of embarrassing stuff about what good men we were and how the Lord would surely reward us. I didn't pay much attention because I was thinking about how small she looked there, even in front of that small cabin, and what a big world it was and how uncaring it can seem sometimes and, if things were different, that could be the woman I'm going to marry standing there or my Ma—and I almost didn't make it back from the war because the Yankees bushwhacked me.

Frank and I rode off just far enough so she couldn't see us. Then we got down off our horses and lay back. Waiting.

"I imagine that banker fellow will be along before too many hours go by," Frank said.

"Yeah, they're always on time when they want their money."

"It's another story when you want to make a withdrawal."

"Yeah, sometimes you just have to let your gun do the talking."

"Lucky we brought ours along, huh?"

Later that afternoon we watched the banker arrive at the widow's place. He was only there a few minutes and when he left Mrs. Settle followed him out onto the porch and said, "It's a beautiful day, isn't it?" but he didn't answer.

A couple of miles down the road, Frank and I approached the banker. Frank nodded at him and said, "It's a beautiful day, isn't it?" but the banker just glared at him.

I pulled my pistol. "I think it's a good day to die," I said. "What do you think?"

"I think you're crazy."

Frank said, "'Life's but a walking shadow, a poor player that struts and frets his hour upon the stage and then is heard no more. It is a tale told by an idiot, full of sound and fury, signifying nothing.'"

"What is that supposed to mean?" the banker asked.

"I don't know," I said, "but my guess is he's trying to tell you to hand over all your money if you want to stay alive."

"I guess I'd be an idiot not to give it to you, but I've always hated parting with things, especially cash."

"You wouldn't need it in the sweet by and by," Frank said.

"I guess I wouldn't at that."

The banker handed us the money and, for a moment, I thought he was going to cry. But he didn't.

I'd thought about taking his watch as a memento, but I settled for getting back the cash we'd given the widow. I don't know why. I guess you don't have to make a profit all the time. You do some things because they're worth doing.

Neither Frank nor I said much as we rode off. I get like that after a job. I need some room to back off from what I've done. To reflect on things. Finally, I said, "Do you really think life's nothing but a tale told by an idiot, signifying nothing?"

"Sometimes it seems that way."

"I refuse to accept that."

"Not accepting something doesn't change the reality of things."

"Sure it does. I've never accepted the fact that the Yanks beat us in the war. Lee surrendered, I didn't."

"You always were one to ride the whirlwind," Frank said.

I wasn't sure what he meant, exactly, but Frank reminds me of a poet Cole Younger told me about. He had a peculiar name—Whit. Cole said he never understood a word the man said and he was always talking. Whit claimed it was one way to find out what he thought.

"You know, Frank. Sometimes I think you missed your calling. You should have been a poet," I said, then I spurred my horse up the slope into the high country.

Frank said I evaporated into the mist when I crested the ridge. I disappeared into the sky. That may not be poetry, but it's magic.

Major, they'll never take me alive, and they'll have to find me to kill me.

Sincerely,
Jesse Woodson James

Kearney
April 25, 1874

Dear Susan,

Zee and I were married by Uncle William yesterday at the home of Zee's sister. About fifty of our friends were present on the occasion.

I know you told me to marry her a long time ago and, probably, I should have but I couldn't until you married Allen and left for Texas.

I'm sorry about the way I behaved last January.

I have my reasons for disliking Parmer, going back to the time we rode with Quantrill, but I shouldn't have invented stories to discredit Allen. I remember I told you about what had happened in Lawrence. I said I saw Allen shoot an unarmed man in the face while his wife pleaded with Allen to spare his life. She and her husband were standing in the middle of the street, I told you, with the town burning all around them. She was hanging onto Allen's saddle, pleading with him. "Please, my husband has never done anything to hurt you. Let him go."

Allen said, "What'll you give me if I do?"

And she said, "Anything. Anything at all."

I told you I'd never forget how relieved she and her husband looked when Allen said, "Maybe we can work something out."

The man was smiling when Allen pulled his pistol and shot him; he said, "That Yankee bastard died happy." Then Allen began laughing while the woman screamed because her husband's brains were all over her face and dress, I told you.

I wasn't at Lawrence.

I'm sorry I made it up, sorry for what I tried that night, but I couldn't stand the thought of losing you. It seemed like my life was ending even though I was only 26. I felt old. *Old.* Maybe I'd just been hunted for too long or maybe it was the morphine I'd been taking... I don't know... but I remember going into the other room and taking the 16 grains I had left. It made me feel... kind of dreamy. When I came back into the room where you and Frank were, it seemed hazy, like somehow fog had crept into the room and I couldn't quite focus on you. I remember sitting in the rocker, moving back and forth slowly, slowly, the floor creaking rhythmically and I said, "I have a story for you." Remember? "About Uncle Jesse."

It seemed like it took me a long time to tell it, that I'd pause for as much as a minute between sentences, but maybe that was the morphine.

I remember saying, "Uncle Jesse was sick for a long time. It seems he'd just get over an illness, then he'd get another, and he finally believed he never was going to be out of pain again—never was going to get well.

"One evening he went out onto the lawn just before it was ready to rain, along about dusk. The clouds were like a giant tarpaulin in the sky.

"Uncle Jesse removed his coat and vest, laying them neatly on the lawn, then he unbuttoned his shirt and lay down on the grass. Then he took his pistol, cocked it, placed it against his heart—and pulled the trigger. Sometimes... I understand why he did that," I said, then I stood up, wobbling, and told you I'd taken the morphine because I didn't want to live to see you and Allen together.

I still don't like Allen but maybe he's good for you. I pray that he is.

If he stands by you the way Zee has stood by me all these years, you'll make it there in Texas—or elsewhere.

You have to understand. Sometimes you're still that

young girl up in the hayloft. Sometimes we're still in the
river together, baptizing each other as the water rushes by
us. I don't want to let you go, even though I know I have to.
Sometimes, suddenly, you're gone and I'm in the river na-
ked and shivering and alone—the way I was when I was
born. The way I'll be when I die.

Love,
Jesse

Sherman, Texas
June 18, 1874

Dear Ma,

We arrived at Susan and Allen's a few days ago, along
with Frank and Annie. A lot of people think Frank and I do
everything together, but I wonder if they'd picture us both
newly married and here together with our wives. We even
went to Galveston together and someone from the paper in-
terviewed us.

I told the reporter the same thing I've told everyone
else, how Zee and I have been engaged for nine years and
how she stuck with me through everything. I said, "You can
say that both of us married for love, and that there cannot be
any sort of doubt about our marriage being a happy one." It
almost sounded like a pronouncement Frank would make. I
guess that's what comes from being brothers.

Frank's wife didn't have the nerve to tell her parents
she was marrying him so Annie wrote her mother. All she
said was, "I am married and going west." Well, Frank can
explain everything later, although he'll use a lot more words
than Annie.

At first I felt uneasy about visiting Susan and Allen
since I was so sure she was marrying the wrong man, since I
tried... you know what I tried. I don't like to talk about it.
But Susan seems happy and in love with Allen and he obviously cares about her so, the second day I was here I said,

"I'm sorry I made such a mess of things. " Then I told Allen, "I can see you've been good to her. I was wrong. What can I say?"

"Nothing. Susan has missed seeing you and Frank. And I'm glad you came, too. You're family now."

I love being married. But after sleeping alone for 26 years it's strange to go to sleep, and to awaken, with some-one by my side. The bed is the same size as the one I've always slept in. I used to feel confined, cramped, but now, with an extra person, the bed seems too big. I want to stay close to Zee. Want to hold her. I don't want any space be-tween us.

I love being married.

I love watching Zee comb and braid her hair, and I keep telling myself, "She's your wife" because it's so hard to believe.

I'll watch Zee making toast or coffee or scrambling eggs or cooking bacon, watch the morning light on her dark hair.

I showed her how to shoot skeet because it gave me an excuse to put my arms around her waist, to put my cheek against hers while I showed her how to lead them through the air. When the clay pigeons shattered she said, "It's like breaking a China plate."

She liked shooting them, but she didn't like the kick of the gun. The next morning her shoulder was black and blue.

"What have I done to you?" I asked, rubbing the bruised area as if I could erase it.

"It's nothing, Jesse. I'm fine."

"Then tell me your name. See if you know that."

"Don't be silly."

"Tell me."

"It's Zee. You know that."

"Zee what?"

"Zee James, silly. Mrs. Jesse James."

"I love hearing you say it. I don't care if it's silly. Every - thing about you makes me happy," I said and I grabbed her around the waist, dancing across the kitchen. I felt like I was 16, not 26. Felt like anything was possible now.

"Stop it," she said. "The bacon will burn."

"Let it," I said, "I don't care," and we whirled around and around the kitchen until we were both dizzy and out of breath.

Love,
Jesse

Sherman, Texas
June 19, 1874

Dear Cole,

Frank and I held up a stage near Austin a few days ago. It was a case of taking from the rich, just like Robin Hood, to give to the poor; we just happened to be the poor.

I said, "I'm sorry to do this, folks, but I know you'll want to make a contribution to my honeymoon fund. Cash and valuables gladly accepted. Just put them in this sack."

One of the passengers was an Episcopal bishop, and he objected to me taking his watch. He said, "I'm doing God's work and have a lot of appointments to keep so I need to know what time it is. How dare you attempt to steal from a man of the cloth?"

"So far as I know, Jesus got by just fine without a watch and a fancy suit of clothes," I said. "Do you think you're better than Jesus? In more need that the Son of the Lord?" You should have seen him squirm. I stuck my pistol in his face and said, "The *Bible* says it's better to give than to receive, so I'd start giving now, you cheap hustler." The people on the coach gasped when I said that.

I considered taking his suit and leaving him there in his underwear (it would probably have been a good lesson in humility) and maybe I would have if you'd been there. I could almost hear your laughter. But you know Frank; he doesn't have much sense of humor, so I just told the bishop,

"See you in Heaven sometime," as we rode off.

See you in Lee's Summit—or Kearney—or Heaven—sometime.

Jesse

1875-1879

Kearney
February 1, 1875

Dear Cole,

We buried Archie in the shade of the only tree in Mt. Olivet Cemetery. It was a bleak, cold day, and the sky had the color of a cast iron skillet.

Less than a week ago, men from the Pinkerton Agency threw a bomb into Ma's house.

Pinkerton's force chartered a special train and came into Clay County at night and crept three miles through the woods to Ma's house and fired it in seven places and hurled the bomb into the house to kill and cripple the entire family and to give them over to the mercy of the flames. But Providence saved the house from being burnt although it was saturated with turpentine and fired with combustible materials. When the bomb exploded, Pinkerton's men fled in the night.

Frank and I weren't home, but Archie had a hole blown in his side, his life leaking away within hours, and Ma had her right arm blown off. Cole, it was as terrible as anything we saw in the war. Worse. At least there a man had a gun— a chance. Here, there was just Ma and Dr. Samuel and their child.

Someday I'll get the murdering bastards.

When Archie's coffin was lowered into the ground, Ma began crying. Until then, she'd managed to stay composed. She said, "I call for vengeance upon the men who did this. He was just a little boy, innocent, who harmed no one. I ask eternal God to look down on me, his mother, to punish these men who set out to harm my family."

After the ceremony, Frank took Ma back to the farm. She was hysterical as he led her up the small knoll from the burial site. She was almost screaming. "Go where he may, Pinkerton's sins will find him out. He can cross the Atlantic but every wave and white cap he sees will remind him of the innocent boy murdered. There is a just God. Pinkerton, I hope and pray our Heavenly Father will punish you for this. I know the spirit of my poor, innocent boy hovers around your pillow, and that you never close your eyes without seeing his poor delicate and childish form about you and him holding his shattered arm over you and you looking at the great wound in his side and seeing his life blood ebb away."

Ma's voice became more and more faint as Frank led her up the small hill, the wind catching her words. She looked like she was a hundred years old. Bent over. Broken.

Zee and I stayed behind. Neither of us had said anything for several moments, then, finally, I said, "Damn it!" even though I almost never swear in front of her. I felt so helpless I didn't know what else to do. In a way I felt it was my fault because I was the one they wanted.

I'll get the murdering bastards.

Zee just looked at me and said, "I know," as if she could read my mind. She put her arm through mine, leaning against me for a long time.

Then we broke a branch from the juniper tree, since it was the only living green thing there, and laid it on little Archie's grave.

Cole, it broke my heart.

Zee said, "Don't cry, Jesse."

"I'm not crying," I said. "It's the wind," but I don't know if it was. "The wind," I insisted.

Neither of us had ever placed a flower, a branch, anything, on someone's grave because we feel you should honor people while they're living, but we didn't know Archie's life was going to be so short. Only eight years old.

The dirty bastards.

There were tears in Zee's eyes as we knelt there. She said, "It seems so unfair, Jesse. So unfair."

We weren't sure why we put the branch of juniper there. We knew it wouldn't bring him back, knew it wouldn't change the circumstances—the inalterability of his death, but....

It was a gesture that somehow seemed important.

                    Jesse

Kearney
April 15, 1875

Mr. Allan Pinkerton:

You and your men have called Frank and me killers, but we've never maimed or killed innocent children.

Frank and I weren't even at Ma's house when your men threw the bomb into it last January. But Ma and Dr. Samuel told us how the bomb exploded, blowing off her right hand and killing little Archie. He was only eight years old.

Now he's buried at the Mt. Olivet Cemetery down the road. Now he'll never know what it's like to get that first kiss or hold a woman. Never.

He lay there screaming, the blood pouring out of a huge hole in his side. Ma tried to help him, but there was nothing she could do. Her right hand hung from her wrist like it was attached by a bloody string and Archie was screaming, "Ma I don't want to die I'm so scared Ma I'm scared," and Ma sat on the floor next to Archie, holding him with her left hand. She said, "Jesse and Frank will get the men who did this," but he didn't hear her.

After the bomb exploded, Dr. Samuel went to the door. On the porch he could hear voices and people were running away in the dark. "Why did you do this?" he yelled, but no one answered.

It took Archie more than an hour to die.

Frank and I know who did it, and we won't forget.

You know who did it: You gave the order.

You've always wanted a confession from Frank and me, even for things we didn't do. Well, here's one I'm going to give you.

Three days ago we went next door to visit Daniel Askew.

He assisted your men the night of the bombing, and he was standing on his porch when Frank and I walked into his yard. It was a cold day but he was sweating. I said. "Couldn't you, at least, have called out to see if Frank and I were there?"

"I don't know what you mean," he said.

"Yes, you do."

"No."

"Why are you sweating so much?"

"I've been working around the farm."

"Sure." I grabbed his right hand, turning it palm up as hard as I could.

"You're hurting me," he cried and he made a funny sound when I twisted his wrist.

"How come you don't have any calluses from the work you do?"

"I... I don't know," he stammered.

I think he was too scared to answer when I asked him if he had a *Bible* or maybe he didn't hear me. "Do you believe in Jesus?"

"Yes, of course."

I said, "Maybe He'll understand how you could maim an old woman and kill an innocent child, you murdering bastard!" and I put my hand on my pistol. "I'll give you one more of a chance than you and the others gave my family. Go for your gun."

"You don't understand... they made me."

"I understand perfectly."

"Please... give me a chance."

"I'll count to three," I said. "That's how long you have to live."

"It was a mistake!"

"I'll say it was... One..."

"We didn't mean—"

"Two."

"—it to happen the way—"

"Three." He was trying to get our the next word when the bullet hit him in the chest. The impact of the slug knocked him back against the door, then he bounced off of it and pitched forward onto his face.

"An eye for an eye," the good book says.

You're next.

Look for me,
Jesse W. James

Chicago
June 1875

Allan Pinkerton:

I killed you yesterday.

You were leaving your office and you stopped to buy a paper from the boy on the street. You paid him, then you stood next to the curb, lighting a cigar, and I had you in my sights.

I smiled, pointing my finger at you, and imagined I pulled the trigger on my Colt.

Bang, the top of your head was blown off.

There was a lot of yelling and screaming and, as people gathered around your body, I quietly strolled away.

I killed you the day before yesterday, too.

You were walking up the steps to your home. When you got to the door, you paused, fumbling for your key. You seemed to be nervous because you took your hand out of your trousers, removing your hat for a moment. Then you grabbed a handkerchief and wiped your forehead with it,

I was standing across the street, wearing "city" clothes. I sighted along my finger and said, "Bang," just as you were putting your hat back on. The bullet took it off, along with the top of your head.

Seconds later, a lady came out from the house. She was crying and when she knelt over you, her dress turned red from the blood.

Tomorrow or the day after or the day after that I'll kill you again. One of those times, the bullet will be real.

I don't actually know why I haven't shot you already. Maybe I want to give you a better break than you gave Ma or little Archie. Or maybe I want you to know I can kill you whenever I want to . Maybe I want you to think about that, to sweat, wondering when the bullet will come.

When you least expect it, I'll be there.

You'll be leaning back lighting a cigar or having a drink at the club with some of your cronies—I think I want to get you when you feel the safest—or out in the park with your wife and kids.

I'll squeeze off two or three fast shots because it will be good to feel the gun buck in my hand.

BANG, BANG.

BANG BANG BANG.

You're dead.

Jesse

Nashville, Tennessee
New Year's Day 1876

Dear Major Edwards.

I've been told I come from a "solitary race."

I don't know if that's true or not but, much of the time, I feel lonely, even when I'm with others, especially if they're not family.

I know how lonely you can be, too. I sensed it the first time we met. You were hung over and you said, "I've just come back from Indian Territory."

When I asked you where that was, I remember you smiled and told me, "It's in the back of my head someplace. When I'm overcome by the routine, the drudgery of day-to-day life, I drink. I confront my demons then. I guess I call it Indian Territory because I go there alone—it's unexplored."

I've spent most of my life in Indian Territory, although I've never drunk much.

Last night, Zee and I had a son, and I never felt more alone that I did while I stood in the other room, waiting for the delivery. I tried to play solitaire but I couldn't concentrate on the cards so I finally went out onto the porch and looked across town. In the distance they were exploding fireworks and it was like orange and green and blue rain coming down on the hills. I watched alone.

I went into the room right after he was born and I sat on the edge of the bed next to Zee, moving carefully. Slowly. Babies seem so terribly fragile.

Zee wanted to name him after me, but we hadn't decided on a middle name. "What'll it be?" she asked.

"I'd like to name him Edwards, after the Major, " I said.

"I like that." Then she handed me little Jesse Edwards and I held him, almost afraid he'd break. So many things in this world do.

It turned midnight just before I left the room and I told Zee, "Happy New Year."

"If you could make a wish, what would it be?" she asked.

"I don't know."

"Ask me what mine would be."

"What would yours be?"

"To stop running. To settle down. To live the way other people do."

"We're not 'other people,' Zee."

"I know that, but I can't help wishing."

"You know what they say about wishing."

"No."

I didn't tell her. Wish in one hand, shit in the other; see which fills up faster. I just said, "It doesn't matter. Nothing matters, except loving you. And little Jesse Edwards being here."

We want you to know how much your friendship has meant to us. You've been there when no one else was and you've always had the words to express what we've felt but haven't been able to say for ourselves. If all men could use words the way you do, they wouldn't have to kill each other. It's the losing man in an argument who punches the other. I've seen men so angry all they could do was say, "Why you...you," and then they'd strike out. With their fists. Or a gun. Or whatever was handy. But they did it because they didn't have the words.

I don't have the words, either, but I recognize the truth in yours.

Happy New Year
Jesse

Dallas, Texas
May 14, 1876

Dear Zee,

Cole sings in the church choir here, and he and Jim have even worked for the sheriff as deputies. It's humorous, but Cole isn't laughing much these days.

Yesterday he had too much to drink and Frank and I had to hold him up when he staggered out onto his porch. When he got there he yelled, "I HAVE TO PISS."

"Not here," Frank said. "The neighbors will see you."

"PISS ON THE NEIGHBORS."

Cole staggered over to the railing, holding onto it with one hand while he unbuttoned his pants with the other. He was singing "Bringing in the Sheaves" at the top of his lungs and peeing.

Frank said, "Watch out, you're hitting your pants," but Cole didn't care.

He stopped singing and said, "Boys, we're pissing our lives away. We could have been anything. Anything." He gestured grandly with both hands, pissing on himself again.

"I saw Belle yesterday," he said and, suddenly, he almost seemed sober. He stopped pissing and stood up straight, wiping at his eyes. I thought he was going to cry, but he just stood there with a faraway look and his voice got softer. "She calls herself the Outlaw Queen now, and she's married to someone named Starr who's nothing but a horse thief."

"Well, we can't live other people's lives for them," Frank said and I thought about my attempt to... end it. You can't interfere with the way someone else wants to live.

"The Outlaw Queen," Cole said again. "You should have seen her. She was riding sidesaddle. She was on Venus and she was wearing a velvet gown and shiny boots and she was holding a pistol. Someone was even taking her picture! It was the damnedest thing. You should have seen her on that horse. The sky behind her was as blue as the rest of our lives."

I said, "She's a good woman, Cole. But you kept leaving her. And. finally, you came around too late. "

"It's too late for all of us. Belle. Me. Pearl."

Then I knew what was wrong with Cole.

"Jesse, she's seven now. And she looks like me. A little. "

"I know."

We sat on the steps and, suddenly, he seemed like a tired, broken old man although he's only three years older than me. He hadn't shaved for a couple of days and his hands shook, and he was getting fat around the middle. For the first time I noticed he had a double chin, and his hair was thinning.

Cole said, "We used to talk about going away together. "

"I know. Belle mentioned it to me once... a long time ago. She said something about the Pacific Northwest and wondered where it was."

"We should have gone, Jess."

"Yeah. Maybe. I don't know. We do what we do, and it's useless to look back."

"You can say that. You and Zee are married and happy and, hell, I don't know. You have it all."

The blue bellies or the Pinkertons or the law have been after me for ten years, so how can I have it all? I don't think I had much of anything until I got you. I know a lot of people have made me into a legend (and I'm not even dead) but they don't know what it's like to have to look behind you everywhere you go. They don't know what it's like moving from place to place, always using a different name until you almost forget your given one. Strangers on the street would kill you (or ask you for an autograph) or do both (ask for your autograph and then kill you) if they knew who you were.

I told Cole, "No one has it all."

"When I talked to Pearl, she didn't even know who I was. I was just some man who was a friend of her Ma's. It almost killed me when she called Sam Starr daddy. I wanted to shake her and say, 'That heathen bastard ain't your daddy,' but what good would that have done?"

92

"Maybe you would have felt better," Frank said.

"I don't think I'll ever feel good again.

"Sure you will," I said. "Sure."

"The only thing that will help me is some more to drink. That's what I need," and Cole stood up painfully and went into the kitchen to get what was left of the bottle.

Love,
Jesse

Dallas
June 1, 1876

Dear Zee,

Cole's probably home by now, and it won't be long before I get back.

We'd planned to return together, but he was dying of a broken heart here. I never believed it, but I think someone actually could die from that.

The day before Cole left he said, "I can't look at Belle... or Pearl without wanting to kill myself. I've go to get out of here."

"I understand, *compadre*." I didn't know what else to say so I put a hand on his shoulder. I thought about telling him it would be all right but I knew he wouldn't believe that and I didn't either. I've never been a good liar.

"If I'm not drunk, I'm trying to get drunk. I know I'm probably killing myself with booze, but I can't stand being sober. Maybe it wouldn't be so hard in Missouri... away from Belle."

"You go back. And leave the bottle here."

"You'll tell Belle I've left?"

When I went to see her, Belle was drunk, too. "It must be going around," I said. "Everyone I know is drinking a lot these days."

"It doesn't have anything to do with you," she said. "Sometimes I think I'm going crazy."

"Maybe we're all a little crazy. Cole was destroying himself... before he left."

"I heard he was gone."

"He wanted me to tell you, I'm sorry I didn't... sooner."

We sat on her porch steps, looking at the dimensionless prairie in the twilight.

"Jesse, what's wrong with us?"

"I don't know. Maybe it's just time catching up with us. We aren't the people we used to be."

The sky seemed to come down like the shade in an unfurnished room and, suddenly, it was dark. Belle said, "I almost killed a man when I heard Cole left."

"What happened?"

"I was wearing my hat with the ostrich feather in it when some bastard started to laugh. He said, 'What do you think you are, a queen?' I'd just crossed the street. 'Yeah, you're a queen,' he continued. 'The queen of cowshit.' I walked away from him, but he strutted along behind me, mincing his words and throwing his hips from side to side, the way some women walk.

"I stopped so suddenly he bumped into me. When I backed off a step or two all I could see was his silhouette against a fiery background and, for the first time, I knew what people were talking about when they claim they see red. 'You son-of-a-bitch, get away from me... now!' I said, but he didn't move. 'Get away.'

"All I could see was red and black and, suddenly, I felt more scared, angry, than I'd ever been so I pulled my gun and I... shot him. It was like I heard the gun go off but someone else had fired it. It was the strangest thing. I watched him fall backward and... Jesse, I could have killed him."

"But you didn't?"

"No, the bullet just grazed him and the doctor came and the sheriff and I was sort of stunned... standing over him. But, my God, Jesse, I shot him because he didn't like my hat!"

"That's not why you shot him."

"I know. But I don't like to think I shot someone because Cole left me."

"He thinks you left him."

"I guess it doesn't matter. He's gone and I'm here. I hate to think about what a botch I've made of my life," Belle said, "and I haven't even begun to live it yet."

I've been described as the most desperate man in America but I didn't feel desperate sitting there with Belle in the enormous darkness. I just felt tired and lonely because I needed to be with you and because I didn't know what to tell Belle and I wanted to comfort her.

Finally, I took out my knife, not saying anything, and started to stick it in the ground next to the toe of my boot, seeing how close I could get. I remember doing that as a kid. Once, I got closer than I meant to and the knife went through the leather into my foot and I ran into the house, screaming, my shoe full of blood. I don't think any of the wounds I've had since then were that terrible.

I miss you.

Love,
Jesse

St. Paul, Minnesota
September 5, 1876

Dear Major Edwards,

I turned 29 today, but I feel older.

After dinner I went out onto the street with Cole and Jim Younger and we walked around town awhile. Cole was expansive because he'd won three hundred dollars playing faro and he thinks the job we're planning up here is going to bring in some big dividends.

"Let's find us a fancy house and celebrate our successes, past and future, along with your birthday," he said.

"You know how I feel about Zee."

"Well, then come along and watch," Cole said and he started to sputter. "You can cheer me on."

"You don't need to be cheered."

"Hell, Jesse, at least you can have a drink. Or a cup of coffee." (I'd told him about my first visit to one of those houses. When the madam asked me what I wanted, I was so scared I blurted out, "I'll have a cup of coffee." I was sixteen.) Cole put his arm around Jim and said, "I'll buy my little brother a piece of poontang unless he wants coffee, too. But it sure isn't what I'm going there for."

"Me either," said Jim.

"I always say a man has to keep it well lubricated, the same way he would his pistol," Cole continued. "I'm always afraid it'll fall off if I don't use it enough."

"I don't think you have to worry," Jim said.

"A man can never be too cautious. Always remember that, little brother."

We walked down the street in the late afternoon sun. When we came to the house Cole was looking for, we went inside. The woman who greeted us looked at me for a moment and said, "Jesse, I haven't seen you in... how long?"

"I guess it's been a decade, Mollie." I introduced her to Cole and Jim, then they went upstairs with a couple of women while Mollie and I stayed in the waiting room.

"You sure I can't find someone for you?" she asked.

"I'm married now."

"Well, that doesn't seem to stop anyone I know. And I get some of the most distinguished men in town here."

"It stops me."

"You always were romantic. You're one of the few people I've ever met who came to a house like mine and talked about love."

"The morning and the evening star. I remember."

"You didn't want just sex, you wanted romance. You wanted music. I always thought you felt cheated because no one was playing the guitar, softly, from some distant corner. "

"I'm one of a kind, all right."

"I don't think most men want sex all that much, at least they don't seem to like it, but they always think they're supposed to so... they come to places like this. Most of them leave in a hurry. As I recall, you always wanted to spend the night."

"Maybe I was just lazy. That's why a lot of people say I do what I do... because I can't hold an honest job."

"I don't believe that."

I shrugged. "What made you leave St. Louis?"

"The Republicans moved in and I moved out. I guess I got tired of hearing about clean living and looking at dirty laundry."

The sun had gradually faded through the red drapes on the front windows and, for a moment, it looked as if the floor was covered with blood, then it was washed away by the darkness. Someone turned the lights on, and a piano began playing in a back room.

Mollie said, "I'll bet you and your wife hold hands."

"Don't embarrass me."

"I think it's nice. I remember you used to come down the stairs with some of the girls... holding hands."

"Now they say I'm a deadly killer."

"I don't care what they say. I know you."

"It's been a long time. A lot of hard riding."

She took my hands without saying anything, looking at them. Then she said, "You haven't changed."

Cole and Jim came down the stairs, laughing. Cole told Mollie, "We brought him here to celebrate his birthday—"

"Happy birthday," she said.

"—but the son-of-a-bitch refused to have a good time."

"I had a fine time," I said, getting up. "It was good talking with you, Mollie."

We said good-bye, then Cole and Jim and I went out onto the porch. The wind had come up and it looked like there were holes in the sky between the stars.

"I'm sorry you wouldn't let me buy you a birthday

bang," Cole said, "but I'll tell you what. I did it twice and had enough fun for both of us." Then he began laughing that big laugh of his and we went back to the hotel to join the others.

Jesse

Sioux Falls, Dakota Territory
October 1, 1876

Dear Zee,

I know you and Ma must have read about what happened in Northfield (people say it's the end of the James-Younger gang). I know you must have spent a lot of nights worrying, wondering if Frank and I were dead in some rainy forest. We just about died.

Everything, at first, was fine. We enjoyed the train ride and we bought some horses in St. Paul.

We thought about taking the bank at Mankato but as I rode up the main street someone who knew me from Missouri yelled, "Hey, Jesse, what are you doing up here?"

I said, "Are you crazy?" I've never seen you before," but I had and I told the boys we had to get out of town.

I guess that's when things started to go wrong.

When we got to Northfield, the First National Bank looked right. Its investors included Ben Butler, a squint-eyed general from the north, and his son-in-law. Butler was one of the most ruthless killers the Yankees had. Right after the war he said, "I want every bastard who fought for the Confederacy to eat dirt for the rest of his life."

On the morning of the seventeenth, the eight of us rode into town. It was sunny but you could feel autumn in the air already that far north.

When we went in that morning to scout the town for the last time, Bob Younger, Charlie Pitts and I had breakfast at J. G. Jeft's restaurant across from the bridge that leads into town. We had a good meal: ham and four eggs apiece, and we left a big tip for the waitress. "Men with our financial prospects can afford to be generous," Bob said, laughing. It was the last time I ever saw him laugh.

It was about 2 p.m. by the time Bob, Charlie and I went over to the bank. Cole and Clell Miller stood out front, watching, and Frank and the other two boys had positioned themselves near the bridge.

When Bob, Charlie and I entered the bank, Bob leapt over the counter. He said, "We're going to rob this bank. Don't any of you holler. We've got forty men outside." If you're going to lie, lie big, Bob always said. He pointed his pistol at the man sitting behind the desk and asked, "Are you the cashier?"

"No."

"The hell you aren't. Open that safe—quick—or I'll blow your head off."

"There's a time lock on," the cashier said. "It can't be opened."

"That's a lie," Bob yelled. He was shaking.

Charlie said, "I'm going to shoot everyone in the place in about a second." There were three employees, including the cashier, who began to scream "Murder, murder, murder" as he ran toward the door. After that, I'm not exactly sure what happened.

Charlie fired his pistol, and someone began shooting out on the street.

Bob turned to one of the other employees and said, "Show me where the money outside the safe is or I'll kill you. "

By now more shots were being fired. One of the windows in the bank was shot out and Cole rode his horse up to the door. "Get the hell out of there," he yelled.

By the time we got outside, Jim's horse had been shot out from under him (it writhed in the street, neighing) but Cole had pulled Jim up behind him. Someone had shot Bob, several times, and he was barely able to stay on his horse. Stiles and Miller were both lying in the street, bloody, neither of them moving.

Cole was covered with blood and he was swearing

senselessly. "Shit, we never should have come here. God-damn it, Jesse." He was wheeling his horse around, trying to get a shot at whoever was trying to kill him, but it was hopeless. Bullets were coming from everyplace. Windows were breaking and you could hear bullets ricocheting and the dust was so thick you couldn't focus on anything. Cole was still wheeling his horse around, dazed, and I saw him jerk in the saddle when another bullet hit him. Jim was just trying to hang on, clutching Cole. Hopeless.

Townspeople were at both ends of the street, firing at us, so all we could do was duck down on our horses and ride through them. As we crossed the bridge, Cole was next to me and he said, "Just a bunch of farmers, huh? Who was the goddamn fool who told us that?"

"Stiles, but it doesn't matter now, " I yelled. "He's dead."

"Great. And we were counting on him to get us out of here."

"We counted on a lot of things."

About fifteen minutes later, the sun disappeared and it began to drizzle.

We went through a couple of little towns with Cole and Jim still riding double, but we managed to steal a horse near Millersburg.

We spent the night in the woods. We couldn't light a fire and we didn't have anything to eat and we were lost. Jim's jaw was almost shot off and Cole figured he'd been shot eleven times, but he wasn't sure. "I never was very good at arithmetic," he said.

"I never was very good at nothin,'" Charlie said. "I guess that's why I rob banks."

"You ain't any good at that, either," Cole said.

"You should talk. You've had everything but your ass shot off."

Frank had been shot through the right leg, but it was a clean wound, and I was hit in the right thigh. I thought I'd just been grazed by the bullet, but it had lodged there.

"Well, where do we go from here?" Bob asked. He was

almost doubled over in pain.

Frank said, "They'll expect us to go south to Missouri. Why don't we fool them and head west?"

It seemed like as good a plan as any. We stuck to the woods as much as possible, traveling slowly; when we met up with a posse on the fourth day, we'd only covered about fifteen miles. We took off through a cornfield, then rode down into a ravine, and we finally lost them. But we were all bleeding and tired and hungry. We ate bugs and berries and, once, we even tried to eat a chicken we stole. We were afraid to start a fire to cook it, though. Cole cut its head off and we cut pieces of its flesh away to chew, but none of us could get it down. Someone was always throwing up.

Progress got slower and slower, and the days got longer. I don't know how Bob managed to hang onto his horse. It was obvious he was going to die.

When we reached the Blue Earth forest I told Cole, "We have to leave Bob behind. He's finished and we will be, too, if we stay with him."

"He's my brother. We can't leave him."

"We've got to."

For the last couple of days we'd had to tie Bob to his horse so he wouldn't fall off. Jim's jaw was swollen and bloody and wasn't connected to the rest of his face properly. And Charlie had several bullets in him.

"Jesse, we've got to stand by each other."

"Bob's going to die. You might as well take your gun and blow his brains out. Put the poor bastard out of his misery. You'd do it for your horse."

"In case you haven't noticed, Bob ain't a horse."

"The man's in agony. Be kind to him."

"Why don't I be kind to you instead?" Cole asked. "I'll blow *your* brains out." He was almost crying.

"If you want me to, I'll... take care of him," I said. "You and the others can ride ahead."

"I don't want to hear about it. Don't say another word, Jesse, or I'll kill you."

Cole was shaking, his face almost purple, and I felt sick. I wasn't going to stay there to be taken alive, and I didn't want to die. "OK," I said. "Have it your way. But I've got to go. Do you understand?"

"I know you've been a friend for a long time. I understand that."

"Let's leave it at that, then," I said, motioning to Frank. "Are you coming with me?"

"Are we brothers?"

We mounted up, not saying anything else. I rode over to Cole, holding out my hand, but he wouldn't take it. "Maybe another time," he said.

"Leave it at that, then," but riding away was one of the most difficult things I ever did.

By the time we reached Sioux City, Frank and I were so stiff we had to mount our horses by climbing onto a fence, then sliding onto them. We were like old men, and I remembered how young I'd felt when we stopped to watch a baseball game on our way to Northfield.

We were in St. Paul and the Red Caps were playing the Winona Clippers. It was the last day of August, less than a week before my birthday. Cole had bet on the losing team and when it looked like someone from the Clippers had hit a home run, Cole shot the ball out of the air. Bang. "I guess that ends the game," he said.

It ended with a bang for us at Northfield.

Love,
Jesse

Dallas, Texas
October 26, 1876

Dear Zee,

It hasn't been six months since I saw Belle, but she looks old for someone who isn't thirty yet. But I should talk. I almost shudder when I look in the mirror. Can that be my face? I ask. I was just a kid, riding with Quantrill and courting you, awhile ago.

Belle's working as a faro dealer in a gambling house here. She said it was either that or kill both of her parents, especially her father, because they always complained about the company she kept. She said, "They claim I'm running with people who are disgracing them."

"You can run with me anytime," I told her. "I guess you know why I've come."

We sat on one of the benches running along the wall, and I kept my back to it.

People were laughing and you could hear the roulette wheel spinning and the sound of chips clicking, and someone wearing a derby was playing the piano in the corner.

"I guess I do," Belle said.

"I thought you'd like to hear it from me. What happened in Northfield."

Her eyes misted over. "You came all this way so you could tell me?"

I nodded. "It was bad, Belle. We never should have gone to Minnesota, but we tried to tell ourselves it would be easy. We'd just be dealing with a bunch of farmers. But Frank and I knew better. And so did Cole. But we got... talked into it, I guess."

"Now Cole's in for life," she said.

"I don't know."

"He *is*, Jesse. A man like Cole. In for life. I'll never see him again."

"Maybe you will. Maybe he'll find a way to get out. He has a lot of friends and there were... circumstances. He mentioned them at the trial."

"I guess hope don't cost anything."

I said, "Things have changed for all of us. It's not like the old days, where I could stay with friends in Missouri or Kentucky and feel safe. Where I knew no one would turn me in. It isn't like that now. The papers are always telling how I've robbed a train, robbed a bank, killed someone. Most of the time I haven't even been to the places they mention but that doesn't matter. The people who read the papers believe everything."

"Lucky more people ain't literate," Belle laughed, then she got serious again. "I thank you for coming here."

"Yeah." I got up, leaning against the wall. The room looked out of focus through the smoke. "I'd better go."

I thought about telling her Cole had won three hundred dollars playing faro when we were on our way to Northfield. At the time we'd all regarded it as an omen, but what could it possibly mean to her?

I wasn't even sure what it meant to me, now, but it was probably the last good luck any of us would have for a long time.

Jesse

Fulton, Missouri
March 2, 1877

Dear Belle,

Ma always told me I couldn't carry a tune, but I've been teaching music at a singing school and giving talks on religion at the local church.

I'm famous for my sermons on the "wages of sin are death" and asking the people in my congregation if they're ready to meet again at the judgment of Him who reads all hearts as an open book. I'll point to someone in church and say, "You may fool your neighbors, you may even fool your pastor, but do you believe you'll fool God and His Son who sits beside Him when it's time for you to enter the kingdom of Heaven?"

I tell you, Belle, I've seen brave men fall to their knees in tears when I say, "Do you think God doesn't know it when you're guilty of usury, when you cheat your brothers? Do you think God doesn't know it when you lust for a woman other than the one you're married to?

"You can fool some of the people some of the time and you can fool a few of the people all of the time, but you can never fool Jesus."

When I teach singing in the Unity neighborhood I stand in front of the group with my baton, waving it and stomping my foot before we begin. "One, two, three," I'll say, then I'll blow into my harmonica and we'll all begin with a favorite like "The Old Rugged Cross" and I think people can probably hear our voices across town, "There's an old rugged cross on a hill faraway," and then we'll sing something like "I Walk In the Garden Alone" and by that time we'll all be stomping our feet and bobbing our heads and maybe sweating if it's a warm night and I always try to end with a few words about the path of righteousness.

It's a good life.

But that's not why I'm writing to you.

A few nights ago I had dinner with Dr. Martin Yates, who's been treating the wound I received in my right thigh when we were leaving Northfield. Martin and I have become friends and he took me to dinner at the Whaley Hotel.

We were seated at a table with several Pinkerton men, including D. G. Bligh. He told us, rather proudly, "I was the first detective hired to hunt the James gang."

"I heard they're desperate men," I said, "especially Jesse."

"Yes," Bligh said, "there's no doubt about it. That one's a killer."

"I don't know," Dr. Yates said. "You hear stories about how he and his brother have done things to help the poor, about how they'll never rob working men or women."

"You'll hear Jesse's a saint, too, but don't believe it," Mr. Bligh said. "What do you think, Mr. Howard?"

That's what everybody calls me here. "I'm so involved with my Bible studies that I really don't follow what's happening in the papers, but you've been looking for the James brothers for... how long has it been? Something like ten years? And you still haven't found them. Isn't that discouraging?"

"Between us," Mr. Bligh said, leaning toward the doctor and me, "we're ready to close in for the kill at any moment now. Jesse and Frank James' days are numbered."

"Is that a fact?"

"It's not only a fact," Mr. Bligh said, "it's a true fact."

"How will you recognize Jesse?" I asked.

"We have a general description of him. He's about five feet, eleven inches tall and he has brown hair and blue eyes. And he's about thirty years old."

"That describes a lot of men," I said. "Why, it could even describe some of us sitting here."

"But none of us have the fiendish look in our eyes that Jesse is said to possess."

"Fiendish look?" I smiled and ordered some apple pie for dessert.

"Fiendish."

"I'd certainly like to be there when you catch him," I said.

"He's vowed to fight to the death," Bligh said. "It'll probably be bloody."

"That wouldn't surprise me at all," I said.

I'm going to send Bligh a postcard saying, "Surprised you didn't note the glint in my eyes when we had dinner at the Whaley Hotel the other evening. (Wasn't the apple pie great?) Maybe next time you'll notice that 'fiendish' look I have, but you'll have to catch me first."

Jesse James

Fulton, Missouri
March 5, 1877

Dear Frank,

The other day I was buying groceries at a small store when I saw someone who looked familiar. Normally, the only faces I recognize are on wanted posters or they belong to Pinkerton men, but I couldn't place this one.

He was telling me one of the most peculiar stories I ever heard. It was about frogs jumping. But it was the way he told it, too, between bursts of tobacco. He'd spit every time he came to a high point and the juice would ring in the spittoon, like a bell between rounds at a boxing match.

He said, "You just have to give some frogs a little tap to get them started. 'Course, others are so dumb they couldn't catch a fly if one landed on their tongue." Bing, he went. "Some of 'em never do take off. There was one frog that just shit on your finger every time you gave it a tap to get it to hop." Bing. "You might as well try to give an elephant an enema as coax some frogs." Bing, bing. He must have thought that line was particularly good.

He finally noticed I was staring at him and said, "What are you looking at?"

I said, "You're Mark Twain, aren't you?"

He nodded and I said, "I guess you and I are about the most famous in our line. My brother says *Tom Sawyer* is one of the greatest books ever written... By an American... At least in this century."

"Please, don't continue," he said. "But tell me something about this literary cricket you have for a brother—and what's your name?"

"Jesse James," I said. "I imagine you know what my line of work is. And don't take offense at any reservations my brother might have about your writing. He hasn't liked much of anything since those plays by Will Shakespeare." Then I gathered up my packages and left.

Jesse

Nashville, Tennessee
February 1878

Dear Ma,

I hate it.

Zee spends most of her time crying, and I don't know

what to say to her. Don't know what to do. The twins meant so much to her, even though we only had them a few days; Zee can't reconcile herself to their loss. Truthfully, neither can I. I keep looking for some passage in the *Bible* that will help me to understand, help me to assuage my grief. But my grief's huge.

Yesterday, I tore a page out of the *Bible*, crumpling it up and throwing it in the yard. Like Job, I wondered how a just God could let things like this happen. Wondered if there even is a God.

I've begun eating my dinner on the back porch so that I don't have to listen to Zee crying. I feel helpless when I'm not able to console her, and I feel guilty when I leave her. But I tell myself she's getting better. Tell myself she'll be all right.

Frank's wife can't produce enough milk for little Robert so Zee has been nursing him with the milk she would have used for our babies. I don't know why, but I'm afraid to say their names.

Zee sits by the window, rocking and crying, rocking and crying, while Annie squeezes her breasts in anguish and says, "It must be God's punishment. I should be the one nursing little Robert. He's my baby. *Mine.*"

Sometimes Frank and I will walk around town, our hands in our pockets. It's dusk and we'll catch people lighting their lanterns, watch the lights come on in Nashville. I think we've walked five or six miles without saying a word.

Sometimes I wonder why anyone has children, but then I think of Jesse Junior's birth. Nothing went wrong there, although it was the strangest New Year's Eve I've ever spent. Wandering around the house, waiting for him to be born. I tried to play solitaire, tried to read. Waiting. I was so befuddled I even tried to play cribbage with myself. Around eleven I heard a cry come from the other room, then the doctor came into the front room and said, "You have a healthy son, Mr. Howard. Congratulations." For a moment I wondered who he was talking to. I've used so many names.

"Happy New Year," I said.

"Yes, I guess it is at that."

Zee and I call little Jesse Tim, and he's never heard us use his given name. He shouldn't have to grow up thinking he's someone he isn't, but the slightest thing could give us away. Zee and I realize that. Even my closest friend here, Dr. Vertrees, doesn't know who I am.

Frank's going to call Robert Mary and put him in a dress whenever he and Annie leave the house with him.

Someday I can hear little Robert insisting, "I'm not a girl. I'm *not*. I'M NOT."

There are a lot of little tragedies no one talks about. The way people lead their day-to-day lives. Sometimes I wonder what's going on inside those houses I pass in the darkness, but I probably don't want to know. There's a lot of pain out there.

Frank tries to deal with his pain by raising his pedigreed hogs (he won first prize for his Poland Chinas at the county fair) and I try to keep busy raising horses. I have some good ones, especially Skyrocket, and I race them at the fair.

Frank says I ought to raise hogs, too, but I tell him, "I hate the dirty things."

"They aren't dirty," he says.

"They look dirty to me," I say, watching them root around in the mud.

Most of the time I don't do anything but look out the window. I'll even go for days without changing my clothes, feeling as dirty as Frank's pigs. But taking a bath, shaving— the smallest things—can seem Herculean. I get nauseated when I try to eat more than a few spoonfuls of anything, and I've quit using salt and pepper.

It's been downhill since Northfield. I can't seem to turn things around.

We rented this house because the trees and tall shrubs in the yard make it difficult for people to look in, but some- times I regret the decision. We have to use artificial light in the middle of the afternoon because no sun comes in.

"It's so dark in here," Zee says. "I want to live someplace where it's always light." Then she'll begin to cry."

I can hear her now, in the other room, crying.

It's time to take a walk.

Jesse

Nashville
midnight, March 1878

Dear Ma,

At night I'm afraid to shut the door to our room. I don't know why, but I feel like I can't breathe when the door's closed. I think I've felt like that since I was a kid, since the time I was sick for weeks and you'd shut the door so people moving around the house wouldn't disturb me.

I thought I was going to die, and I guess I still feel shut in when I'm in a room with a closed door.

Sometimes Zee awakens in the night, and she'll shut the door to keep out intruders even though she knows no one will get into the house. Those are the times I'll wake up sweating,

I woke up a few minutes ago, perspiration dripping from my face, my pillow as wet as if someone had thrown a glass of water on it. I sat up in the dark, trying to breathe. "Why'd you shut the door?" I asked Zee.

She sat beside me, leaning back against her pillow in the darkness. "I heard noises downstairs."

"It's just your imagination."

She said, "I thought I heard the twins crying."

"Zee, the twins are dead."

She didn't say anything for a long time, and I almost thought she'd fallen asleep sitting up. I almost wished I had a cigarette to smoke—or a cigar—although you know I've never used tobacco. But it would have given me something to do. Lighting up.

"Do you think the dead know what time it is?" Zee asked.

I didn't know what to say to that. I put my left arm

around her. Finally, I said, "Why don't I make you a glass
of warm milk? Maybe it'll help you sleep."

"Yes, maybe it would. I'd like that."

I came downstairs a few minutes ago, pouring the milk
into a pan and building a small fire in the stove. There were
still a few warm coals left from dinner so it didn't take too
long for the fire to catch.

While the milk was warming, I went out onto the back
porch. It was cold out but the sky was as clear as I'd ever
seen it and I tried to find the constellations.

I remember Dr. Samuel showing them to me when I
was a child. He'd say, "That's Cassiopeia's chair. And
there's the Big Dipper. And the Little Dipper."

I remember there was also a lion and a pitcher and a
hunter but I don't remember their names anymore and I
couldn't find them, even though I looked up into the sky
until my neck was sore.

By the time I went back into the house the milk was
boiling and I poured Zee a glass full and watched her drink
it. Then we lay back down and I held her, neither of us
saying anything. (I did learn to go a long time without talking when I was sick.) Finally, I felt her body relax and I
knew she was sleeping.

I lay there telling myself the Lord is my shepherd I
shall not want I will lie down beside green pastures the Lord
is my shepherd I shall not lie down beside the Lord, jum-
bling the words, and I got up and came back downstairs.

Love,
Jesse

Nashville
May 12, 1878

Dear Frank,

I almost killed a man today.

I was in Dood Young's blacksmith shop, having some

of the horses shod, when Dood came in drunk. He thinks everyone who wasn't born here came from Ohio. He said, "You goddamn Yanks think you can come down here and take over."

"I hate the blue bellies as much as you do," I said. "I fought against them."

"What regiment were you with?" he asked.

I was afraid to tell him I rode with Anderson and Quantrill because it might give me away. Everyone here knows me as Thomas Howard.

"Maybe you don't remember," he said. "If there's anything I hate worse than someone from Ohio, it's a liar."

"I'm from Missouri, and I'm not a liar."

I've seen Dood break a two by four with his fist. If he swung at me, I knew I'd have to kill him. I told myself: I have to keep my temper. Have to... think of Zee. I promised we wouldn't move again. Wouldn't run.

"Then why won't you tell me who you rode with?"

I understood why I've used a gun to solve a lot of problems. You just can't argue with some men. Reason won't work. Words, at least mine, fail. I've tried to go straight. To do things the way you're supposed to.

I was cheated out of several hundred dollars in a grain deal by a man named Johnson earlier this year, and I even hired an attorney to get my money. I promised Zee, "I'll do things the right way. The way you want me to."

"You'll see," she said. "The law won't let a man like Johnson cheat us."

"I'll believe in the law the day I get a check," I told her. "Or the day after I deposit it and it doesn't bounce."

I've been trying to get my money since January and I'm tired of waiting. I told Zee, "It'd be a lot easier to stick a gun in Johnson's face. He'd see the light in a hurry."

"Jesse, that's how you've done things all your life."

"It's worked, hasn't it?"

She began to cry. "How can you say that? Look at us. We're lucky to stay in a place for a year and we've never

been able to use our real names. I'd like to live the way
other people do. I'd like to go into a store and tell the people
I'm Mrs. Jesse James. I'd like to be able to play cards with
friends and not have to worry about forgetting to call you
Tom or Mr. Howard."

"You knew how it would be when you married me."

"Yes, I knew," she said. Then she slumped onto the
couch and began to cry. I guess men hit each other when
they don't know what to say and women cry. It's the same
thing.

I just felt tired when I watched her. Felt tired when I
tried to get the money Johnson owes me. Felt tired again
when I walked out in front of the blacksmith shop with
Dood. I seem to spend a lot of my time feeling tired lately.
Sometimes I don't want to get out of bed in the morning.
The day seems heavy. Oppressive. Sometimes I feel like that
guy who had to push a boulder uphill for eternity.

I told Dood part of the truth. "I rode with Quantrill.
And Anderson."

"Then you must have known the Youngers. And the
James," he said.

I nodded.

"Tell me about them."

"Some other time," I said. "I really can't now." I
thought he was going to ask why not, but he didn't. He just
leaned toward me, and I could see how bloodshot his eyes
were. "I'm not sure why, but I believe you," he said.

"I'll tell you this: I know Jesse better than I do my own
brother."

"Well, I consider myself lucky to know you then."

"You're luckier than you think," I said. He didn't know
how close he'd come to dying.

Jesse

Hot Springs, New Mexico
Saturday night
July 26, 1879

Dear Zee,

   At dusk the sky is as thin as paper here and it's hard to breathe, perhaps because the air is as thin as the sky. I lay on my bed in the ruined twilight, then I walked out onto the verandah. The clouds scudded across the sky like great, prehistoric birds beating their mad wings.

   I mixed some morphine and water, but I don't know if I took it because of my wounds or because I thought it would make me less lonely as I stood out there beneath that gigantic sky, so far away from you. I remembered the way you used to stand near the windows of our bedroom at night, combing your hair, the moonlight highlighting your breasts. I'd come up behind you and you'd always pretend you didn't hear me, but I knew you did. I'd put my arms around your waist, my hands just touching your breasts. All you'd say was my name, "Jesse." Whispering it.

   Then the twins died and you didn't stand by the windows anymore. No matter how hot it was you'd tell me, "I feel cold. I *always* feel cold." But when I put my arms around you so you could share my warmth, you'd move away from me. And I died a little each time you did that.

   No matter how much light there was in the house you'd say, "It's dark in here. *Dark.*" And you'd light all the lamps in the middle of the afternoon.

   When we went out for walks in the evening you'd say, "I'm drowning in the darkness. I want to go back," and you'd stumble as if you were blind but I almost liked the pain you must have been feeling because you'd touch me.

   I know I'll hold you again. When the new baby comes, everything will be the way it used to. I know that.

   We'll stand on the balcony together, watching the sky unfurl itself along the mountains like a rose. And we'll watch the stars hurl themselves against the dark hills until they disappear the way we all will, finally.

I read that someone in Montana built a cabin out of dinosaur bones. I don't know why he did it, but it must have something to do with the way we live our lives, trying to reconstruct the past, to hang onto it, even as we destroy the future. Here's this lonely sheepherder, preserving these bones so we can remember what those huge beasts were like while other men do their best to kill the last of the buffalo.

Frank, in a pensive mood once, asked, "Why should we live when we know we're going to die?"

I couldn't answer him then, and I'm not sure I can now. But it has something to do with the stars and holding someone you love in the enormous darkness.

I wish you were here so I could hold you now.

Jesse

Hot Springs
July 27, 1879

Dear Zee,

Nothing is green here. Nothing seems to be alive.

There's some scrub brush and cactus and the mountains in the distance that turn plum colored in the twilight, but I've yet to hear a bird sing.

I'm sorry to be gone while you're pregnant, and I keep wondering if I'm a father again. If I were the kind of man I'd like to be, I'd be there with you; I know that Frank and Annie will do everything they can for you, but a man ought to be with his woman.

I know you want a girl this time, so I hope you get one. I also know how scared you are that something will go wrong again; I suppose neither of us will ever forget the twins. Gould and Montgomery would have been a year old now, but the only thing we have to remember them by is our pain, as if we need more of that. I've been shot at for half a lifetime.

I realize we can't go back to Missouri and Tennessee is getting more dangerous for us each day. Sometimes I think there isn't a place left for us.

This afternoon Moore and his wife made a big dinner for me. Moore hasn't changed a lot since he and I were kids in Clay County. He's still shy—he lets his wife run things at the hotel here—although he came running toward me when I arrived. At first I thought he was going to hug me but he stopped, suddenly, a couple of feet in front of me, looking kind of abashed, then he stuck his hand out and said, "It's good to see you, Jesse." Of course he introduced me to the other guests as Tom Howard.

I sat down to dinner with Dr. Hoyt and Miguel Antonio Otero, the former governor of New Mexico, and before we'd finished the first course a young fellow dressed in black came over to our table and joined us. He said, "I know who you are. Moore has told me about you."

When I said, "Yes, I'm Tom Howard," he smiled and told me he was William Bonney.

The Kid had Moore bring him a glass and some whiskey and by the time we'd finished dinner, he'd consumed half the bottle.

He never stopped talking. He killed his first man when he was 12 and, a couple of years later, he claims he killed a Negro who cheated at cards and called him "Billy Goat." Listening to him, it was hard to tell what he'd invented from what he'd done. Probably he doesn't know himself. No one has to tell me how hard it is to separate the man from the myth.

As the Kid drank, he talked more and more about how much the senoritas like him, and when a Mexican woman came into the bar he put an arm around her, asking if she'd like a drink. When she refused, he began laughing and said, "Hell, have one anyway," and he tipped the bottle so that the whiskey poured out over her face and down her blouse.

At first she just laughed but when Billy poured more

whiskey on her, she began coughing and tried to pull away from him. She said, "Stop that, Billy, stop it," but it was as if he'd gone crazy. He began laughing, pushing himself against her—she was backed into the bar—and he ran his hands over her body. She was beginning to tremble when I got up from the table and said, "That's enough, Kid."

His hand dropped to his gun when he turned toward me. It was as if he had trouble focusing on me for a minute, as if he couldn't remember who I was. It was like he was looking at a blurry photograph. He said, "Look, grandpa, I didn't ask for your advice."

"I didn't mean to butt in," I said, "but the senorita doesn't seem to be having such a good time. Why pick on her when there must be a lot of them around here who couldn't keep their hands off of you?"

I can't imagine *any* woman, Mexican or white, letting herself be touched by him, but he's vain, he thinks the world loves him, so I appealed to his vanity. He's the kind of man who must spend an hour looking into the mirror each morning. Nothing about him's careless. Even the way a few strands of hair fall across his forehead, as if they were blown there by the wind—planned, all planned.

Billy pushed the woman away from him, his face brightening, and he said, "Can't keep their hands off—yeah," then he grabbed the bottle and almost spun around toward the door. The Kid always seems to be running, even when he isn't. Maybe it's the way he throws his hips, almost like one of the senoritas he's always after, when he walks.

As Billy went out, the light reflected off his guns and the bottle of whiskey so that it looked as if he were on fire—he said, "So long, Mr. Howard," without turning around—and, for a moment, I was sure he was drowning in flame.

Love,
Jesse

Hot Springs, New Mexico
July 28, 1879

Dear Belle,

I don't think I've ever met anyone more intense than
Billy the Kid.

He was in the bar this morning, playing with a knife.
He said, "You know how a bat never flies into anything,
even when it's flying in the dark? Well, I can see my fingers,
even with my eyes shut."

Billy spread the fingers on his left hand, shut his eyes
and held the knife in his right hand. "Now," he said, "count
as fast as you can. Each time you say a number, I'll stab the
table, bringing the point of the blade down between one of
my fingers."

"You don't need to prove anything."

He looked up at me for a second, saying, "Just do it,"
then shut his eyes again.

"This is senseless."

"*Do it.*"

I could see he wasn't going to quit, so I began counting,
"One, two, three." Each time I pronounced a number, he
brought the knife down between one of his fingers. It was
uncanny, the way some people can handle cards, turning up
any one you ask for from the deck. But this was dangerous.

I started to count faster but he kept up with me, the
blade biting into the wooden table top. "One," bunk, "two,"
bunk, "three." Bunk bunk bunk, the blade bit into the wood,
and Billy's hand seemed to blur.

By the time I'd counted to twenty we were both sweating. I said, "We'd better stop now."

He looked up at me like a blind man, like someone in a
coma. He saw me, but he didn't see me. I think he was
looking at something inside himself. His face was almost
translucent.

If he'd gone out into the sun, I don't think he'd have
cast a shadow. There was something unreal about him. He
wasn't quite there for a moment but, gradually, I watched

him come back. "That's quite a trick," I said, but I don't think he heard me.

Jesse

Hot Springs, New Mexico
July 29, 1879

Dear Frank,

Sometimes the sky is reflected onto the land out here so it looks as if there's water ahead of you, but it keeps receding as you approach it, and a lot of men have died of thirst, their arms reaching out for something that isn't there.

I don't think anyone has ever reached the Kid, either. He's popular with the senoritas and you'll see him in the bar, laughing and drinking with the other men, but he's never quite there.

You and I know what it is to see men die, but I've never seen anyone with the look of death in his eyes before. The Kid has it. He says men have tried to kill him at point blank range, so close they couldn't have missed, and he's convinced the bullets have gone through him.

When we were out riding after dinner at the Old Adobe Hotel last night, he suddenly reined his horse in, dismounted and said, "Shoot me."

I just looked at him like he was crazy—he *is* crazy—in the late afternoon light. Earlier, he'd showed me how fast he is with a gun, fanning his pistol at a cactus. He shot the top of it off, then rubbed the water inside it onto his face. In the twilight it seemed to make his skull glow. It was eerie because he was dressed in black, his body blending into the darkening mountains behind him.

"I don't want to kill you," I finally said.

Billy started to, I don't know, kind of dance there in the desert. It was as if he heard some music I didn't and moved with an invisible partner, then he began singing some song I'd never heard before. He stopped moving, fading away again, his skull glowing. "Shoot me, old man. Bullets can't hurt me."

I guess 31 does seem old when you're 19.

"Did they shoot off your balls at Northfield?" he asked. "Maybe you ought to take me back to Missouri so I could help you out with your wife."

His voice was high, squeaky, and if you listened to him long enough, you could almost hear a little kid yelling that he'd lost his toys, but this Kid's dangerous. Quirky. He can change in a minute.

I thought about shooting him. Probably it wouldn't be such a bad idea, but I couldn't do it then, there. Not like that. But there are a lot of people around here who'd like to see the Kid dead. It won't be long before someone pulls the trigger.

Jesse

Hot Springs
July 30, 1879

Dear Frank,

I saw the Kid again today, and I know one thing: I've got to get out of here or I will be the one to pull the trigger. It's almost as if he wants me —or someone—to kill him. Maybe he's so miserable that dying seems preferable to living, although he's always laughing. But it's a strange, hollow laugh without any joy in it.

His eyes never laugh. Even when he's dancing or hugging one of the Mexican women who always seem to be around him, his eyes are empty. And for three days in a row, he's worn black, as if he's going to a funeral. I don't know if he owns more than one suit of clothes.

This afternoon Moore and I were having a beer in the bar when the Kid came in. He stood about ten feet down the bar from us, ordering whiskey, then he said, "You've been going downhill ever since Northfield. What you need is some new blood."

"Someone like you?" I asked.

"I'd do."

"Why would you want to hang around with someone who's going downhill?"

"Maybe I'm a good Samaritan."

"Maybe my dog would mistake your leg for a tree and piss on it."

I could tell Moore was getting nervous; he said he had to go into the kitchen to see if his wife needed any help. Moore never was long on courage.

"What are you trying to say?" the Kid asked.

"Maybe you're the one who's going downhill."

"At least I'm not running away. New Mexico is my territory. It's where I belong."

The windows and doors to the hotel were open, but it must have been more than a hundred degrees in there. We were both sweating. Out on the street, someone was playing a mournful love song on the guitar, and I suddenly missed Zee. Suddenly missed Missouri. I knew you and I didn't want to try ranching here. These people are different from us somehow.

I said, "Some people will think you're afraid to leave home."

"The people here all know me. They see me riding down the street and they'll point me out: 'That's Billy the Kid,' they'll say. I don't have to hide behind another name, like some people do. When they see me, they know something exciting's going to happen. I'm going to grab one of the senoritas and we'll dance or make love."

"I've always been a family man."

He almost sneered when I said that. "Family, huh? I'll show you family," and he took his pistol out of its holster, stroked the barrel slowly, the light glinting on it, then holstered the gun again. For a moment I thought he was going to try something. "That's my family," he said, "and *that*," touching the buttons on his pants.

"Am I supposed to be impressed?"

"People around here are. I'm 19 and I'm already a legend."

"I rode with Bill Anderson during the Civil War. I was 17 and I saw a lot of snot noses like you. Now they're all dead. "

"Yeah? Well, I ain't dead, *Mr. Howard*. There're close to 20 men who wish they'd never met me. At least they'd wish that if they were still alive. " And he laughed that funny, toneless laugh, tossing off a shot of whiskey in one gulp. His face flushed and he pushed back his hat. Then he took a long slug of whiskey from the bottle. "You know, you and I ought to be friends," he said. "We could do something big."

"Like what?"

"Shit, I don't know. But I haven't had many laughs since I broke out of the Lincoln jail. I let Deputy Ollinger have it with both barrels of his own shotgun. When I was making my break, he was out in the street and I yelled, 'Hey, Ollinger. Here's a present for you.' Then I waited a couple of seconds so he'd know who I was. The last thing he ever said was, 'Don't do it. Kid.' After I pulled the trigger, I whooped and hollered, dancing around the bastard's body for almost an hour. "

"I don't think there's anything funny about killing people. "

"Don't get sanctimonious with me. I know what kind of a man you are."

I think the Kid believes everyone enjoys killing the way he does. He wouldn't understand it if I tried to tell him you and I didn't have the choices he did. He robs and kills because it's easier than working. I thought about telling him that you and I didn't have any choice because we rode under the black flag during the war. The Yanks never forgave us. Thought about telling him you and I are tired of running, that we'd just like to have a small piece of land we could farm and maybe get us a few horses. I thought about telling him we never rode with people like him, but he wouldn't have known what I was talking about.

I'm coming home tomorrow—this place isn't for us— and the Kid is going to go on with what's left of his life here. Nothing will change that. I said, "Billy, I guess you do know what kind of a man I am at that. Let me buy you the next drink."

"Now you're finally starting to make sense," he said, and, God pity him, he believed it.

See you soon.
Jesse

Hot Springs
Thursday, July 31, 1879

Dear Zee,

Probably, I saw the Kid for the last time this morning.

He wavered a little, hung over, or maybe it just seemed that way because of the wall of heat around us. His face seemed as soft as butter.

It isn't hard to imagine the Kid and me facing each other down, but I'll let the pulp novelists describe that scene if they ever discover we've met. They won't hear it from me.

I don't know if the Kid has spasms or not, but this morning his hands were almost fluttering and I remembered watching some hummingbirds, their wings blurring as they hovered over a red fuchsia. The Kid's hands seemed to blur like that.

Just before I got on the stage Billy said, "Sorry to see you go," offering me his hand. It was limp, feminine, and I almost had the feeling that a woman had come out in men's clothes, posing as Billy, but it was him all right.

When the stage pulled out, I thought about waving goodbye, but I didn't. I almost had the feeling the Kid would turn into a pillar of salt (I could taste the salt on my lips) if I turned around. Maybe I should have done the world a favor and looked back.

Love,
Jesse

Nashville
August 7, 1879

Dear Ma,

Soot colored clouds smudge the denim sky, and everything seems gray, even the rain.

Zee says the sky's the color of an unwashed vest.

We thought about moving to New Mexico, but when I came back from there I told Zee, "It isn't right for us."

She said, "You know where you want to be," and she didn't have to tell me.

I've been hunted like a wild animal from state to state. I've known no home, and I've slept in all sorts of places. Here today, there tomorrow. I've been charged with every crime committed in Missouri or in her neighboring states. If they don't kill me for something I've done, they'll kill me for something they've imagined. I've been taught to suspect my nearest and dearest friends of treachery.

I don't know where it will all end.

I'm tired of this life of taut nerves, of nightriding and dayhiding, of constant listening for footfalls, cracking twigs and rustling leaves and creaking doors. Tired of seeing Judas on the face of every friend I have, and God knows I have none to spare. Tired of the saddle, the revolver and the cartridge belt.

I've had enough of exile. I want to come home.

Jesse

Nashville
August 10, 1879

Dear Frank,

I came home to find Zee and the baby.

I looked at her and asked, "What'll we name her?"

"Why don't we call her Mary," Zee said, "after the mother of Jesus?"

"Maybe the name will help to protect her. It's been a

long time since anything went right," and I thought about Gould and Montgomery dying last year, thought about how long it had taken us to come to terms with our grief. That's one reason we decided not to name Mary until we knew she was going to live.

I wasn't sure I wanted another child but Zee said, "I think we should have one" late last fall when it seemed like everything was dying, even the mountains.

"After what happened?"

"*Especially* after what happened." Then Zee said something that I thought about for a long time. "The sun sets, but the light doesn't fade."

That evening, going out for a walk, I watched the sun disappear like a wafer dissolving in water (the sky seemed effervescent) and I knew, somehow, Zee was right, although I wasn't even sure what she meant.

It reminded me of something you said after what happened in Northfield: "We're burning in water and drowning in flame." I thought about that a lot, too.

I want to thank you and Annie for looking after Zee while I was gone. Sometimes I think Zee and Jesse Junior are the only reasons I have to live. And, of course, now there's Mary.

Not that it matters, now, but I don't think I'll ever understand Cole. He and Belle were as good a couple as most people ever get to see, but he couldn't seem to settle down. Couldn't seem to love one woman.

I never told you this, but the day I turned 29 when we were heading toward Northfield, Cole won three hundred dollars playing faro. He insisted on buying me a birthday drink I didn't want, but I didn't want to refuse him, either. He was feeling so happy.

Cole had two or three drinks to my one, then he said, "Jesse, there're a lot of good looking women around here, and I'm going to get my wick dipped. Why don't you come along?"

I knew Cole meant well, but it kind of made me angry.

"You know how I feel about Zee," I said.

"What she don't know won't hurt her. And if you don't say anything, I won't either. I'll tell you what, since you're a friend and you're damn near an old man now—I'll even pay for any girl you want. You'd better get it in while you're still able to get it up."

"You go ahead, Cole. I have some thinking to do."

"You're the only man I respect who'd turn down a piece of ass," he said, following me out onto the street. He was still jabbering as we walked toward the whorehouse. I thought a fool needed company (I waited for him downstairs) but I'm glad he went now. I imagine that was the last woman he'll ever sleep with.

Cole never was very good at being alone, and I imagine it's plenty lonely in that cell in Stillwater. I think about him and Jim and Bob a lot. The only way they'll ever get out is to be carried out... *The sun sets, but the light doesn't fade.* I wonder if Cole and Jim and Bob believe that.

If you ever hear they've taken me alive, say it's not true. They can kill me but they'll never get me otherwise.

Love to you & Annie
Jesse

Nashville
November 22, 1879

Dear Susan,

George Shepherd, who did a couple of jobs with us, claims he killed me but Robert Pinkerton says, "I don't believe Shepherd would dare to shoot at him." Pinkerton also says, "I consider Jesse James the worst man in America." (He just doesn't know me.) "He is utterly devoid of fear, and has no more compunction about coldblooded murder than he has about eating his breakfast."

Shepherd claims he went to Ma's house, where someone blind folded him and lead him to our camp in the woods. (I think he's read too many dime novels.) Shepherd went on to say we were going to rob a bank in Short Creek, near Joplin, but we decided not to because we saw a guard stationed there. As we were riding through the woods, Shepherd turned on me, pulling his gun. I also drew mine, but he fired first, and the bullet hit me behind the ear. He says I was dead before I hit the ground.

The only way Shepherd (or anyone else) will get me is in the back.

"What do you know? They've killed me again," I told Zee when I read the article. I couldn't help laughing.

"Who did it this time?" Zee asked.

"George Shepherd."

"I thought he was in jail in Kentucky."

"I guess someone made the mistake of letting him out."

"He must be desperate to get his name in the papers," Zee said.

"A lot of men who've ridden with me live in my shadow, and I can understand their not liking it. But I hate liars."

"They think what you've done takes something away from them."

Zee poured me some coffee and I set the papers down. "That's why I miss Cole so much," I said. "He was his own man. He's never said a bad word about me... not even after Northfield. And I know he felt I betrayed him there."

"You've never betrayed anyone. There or anywhere else."

"Tell that to Cole. To a lot of people."

That night I couldn't sleep. I lay there in bed for a long time, then I got up and went into the other rooms to see how the children were. I looked at them in the moonlight coming through the window.

God, I hope they never have to pay for what I've done. For who I am. Frank quotes somebody, saying, "I am what I am and they that level at my abuses reckon up their own." That sounds nice but they're just words. I felt sad standing there.

I put on my clothes and went outside. I could see my breath in the air, and the moon looked like someone had sprinkled it with phosphorus.

I thought about what I'd read in the papers. Even though I'd laughed about it, reading about my death gave me a strange feeling, and I suddenly began to shiver.

It's just the cold, I told myself, it's just the cold, but I've never been a good liar.

Jesse

1880-1882

Nashville
May 20, 1880

Dear Susan,

You remember how I always used to laugh, to take chances, to be daring? Like a lot of young people, I was convinced nothing could harm me.

Am I growing old?

Now life seems tragic to me. Zee and I lost the twins, then a grain deal went bad. I thought we might be able to turn our lives around in New Mexico, but it was a dream, like the one Belle had about her and Cole going to the Pacific Northwest. Like our California dream.

Now I look both ways before I cross the street and I often have the feeling someone's following me. I'll go around a corner and flatten myself against a wall, my hand on my pistol, waiting... So far, all I've managed to do is scare an old lady.

I never laugh anymore.

It's been more than three years since Northfield, but I'm still haunted by what happened there. I see Jim coughing up blood, even with my eyes shut, and Cole holding the reins with one hand and his guts in with the other.

I have to end the dream.

Last month I decided to rob a bank again, and I got a couple of men to go with me. But when we arrived, there must have been a dozen people inside, and I could see they were armed.

Had one of the men talked about our plan?

I don't trust anyone except Frank anymore. He's rented some land on White Creek, a few miles from here, and he must spend ten hours a day in the fields.

I told him, "There's a bank in Empire City with a lot of money in it. We could take it. Easy."

"Nothing's easy, Jesse."

"This is. And it must have a hundred thousand dollars in it."

"Think about what happened at Northfield."

"That was over three years ago."

"Tell that to Cole. And Jim. And Bob. They're still in jail."

"Cole was a fool. He could have come with us." We were in the woods and we sat on the stump of one of the large trees Frank had cut. "Jesse, I like farming. It's what I am: a farmer."

"Then come with me because you're my brother. I'm running out of money, and I need your help. I'm asking you."

"You should have learned your lesson at Northfield. We could be cut down like... this tree," Frank said. He opened a bottle of beer he'd brought with his lunch. "You said there wouldn't be anymore banks. Ever."

"I've never asked you for much. But - I'm - asking - now. Help me."

I got up, walking around the stump Frank sat on. I walked faster. Talked faster. I felt like knocking the bottle out of his hand. I could feel myself going. The light came through the trees, dizzying me. "I wouldn't turn you down," I said.

"I wouldn't ask you to rob a bank."

"Just this one last job," I said. "It would get me back on my feet."

"You said it was going to be our last job when we robbed that train last year in Jackson County."

"I thought it would be, but the payroll wasn't as big as I expected. Remember?"

"We each got more than a thousand dollars. What'd you do with your share?"

"I don't know. Damn it, does it matter?" I could feel the muscles in my neck tightening, feel another one of those headaches coming on. They come at me behind the eyes. I can even feel the pressure against my teeth.

Frank stood up, taking a sip of beer. Somehow, he'd never seemed more sanctimonious. "I'll loan you some money... if that will help."

"I don't want your damn charity," I said. "I don't want anyone's charity."

"You're my brother."

"Don't tell me that when I'm dying and you won't help me."

"Jesse, you're not dying." He put a hand on me, trying to get me to stop, to slow down. I was walking faster, but I was just going in a circle.

I slapped his hand away. For a moment I think I went crazy. I didn't even know who he was. I just saw his silhouette in the light and I kept blinking. Blinking rapidly. Trying to bring things into focus. I grabbed my pistol to... I'm not sure what I was going to do.

Frank brought the beer bottle down on my wrist—hard—and I dropped my Colt. It lay there in the dirt at my feet and when I bent over to pick it up, I was panting. I thought I was going to pass out. I was sweating, even though it wasn't a hot day. "I... I...."

"It's OK, Jess."

"It's not OK, it'll never be OK," I said. And I ran across the field, stumbling and falling because I couldn't get things into focus.

When I got home Zee looked at my hands and said, "They're bleeding, Jesse. What did you do?"

"I don't know. I was talking to Frank and...." I shrugged. Zee picked the small pieces of dirt out of my palms, washing my hands gently, then she rubbed salve into them. I'd even cut my forehead and when she washed that, her hair touched my face and I was almost sane again.

I know I ought to see Frank—or write to him—but I keep seeing that bottle coming down on my wrist, keep seeing my Colt falling... slowly... into the dirt. It's like a dream I have.

I'm at the bottom of a shaft. I can see the light at the top and I'm trying to climb back up... but I keep slipping. Just as I'm about to get to the top, the ground gives way and I'm falling... falling... my voice echoing around me.

When I awaken, I'm shouting, "Frank. Frank."

Love,
Jesse

Nashville
June 4, 1880

Dear Belle,

This is what I've been reduced to: riding with horse thieves. I've known Jim Cummings since the war, but he's sullen and stupid. And there's a stale smell about him. Maybe he kept his clothes in a trunk in the basement for a long time, and he can't wash the musty smell out of them. I don't know.

At the end of a day's ride, most men will dismount, slapping the dust from their clothes, their bandannas over their noses to keep the dust out. But Cummings seems to absorb the dust. It sticks to his skin. He's always sweating, and he says he hates summer.

I miss Cole's loud laugh. His wit. His intelligence. I wish I could see him again. There's a line Frank loves to quote from *Hamlet*. Hamlet's talking about his father, who's been murdered, and he says, "He was a man, take him for all in all. I shall not look upon his like again." Shakespeare must have known a man like Cole.

I shall not look upon his like again.

Probably Cummings can be trusted, but he's dull. He was here a few days ago, hovering like a blue bottle fly. When Jim and I went to Warner's Restaurant, I waved at a local constable named Watson. He's as fat as a Christmas turkey and if he had a white beard, he'd look something like Santa Claus.

I grabbed Jim's arm and said, "Let me introduce you to our local constable."

"Not by a damn sight," Jim said. "Do you think I'm a fool?" He backed toward the door. "Sometimes you don't have no sense, Jess."

"It's Howard," I said. "Tom Howard. Don't ever forget that."

"I don't care what you call yourself. Someday your brashness is going to get you killed."

"Someday you're going to wake up dead if you don't watch your tongue. You know what I mean?"

Jim just stood there, sweating and looking stupid. He scratched his head a moment, then asked, "How can I wake up if I'm dead?"

I said, "The best way to get arrested is to sneak around. I have a lot of important friends here. One of them's even a legislator."

"I'd still like to know how I can wake up if I'm dead," Cummings said. "I don't know why I hang around with someone who don't make no sense. And I don't like the way that constable is staring at me neither," he added, almost running out of the restaurant.

I walked across the room, brash as sassafras, to where Watson was sitting and said, "I'm thinking about entering my best horse in the four mile race coming up in Louisville. Do you think he has a chance?"

"If Skyrocket can run as fast as that friend of yours who just left he's a sure winner," Watson said and we both began to laugh.

Love,
Jesse

Emerson County, Kentucky
September 3, 1880

Dear Frank,

More and more, I live in memory. What happened to me a decade ago is more real than what happened today. I'm an anachronism, like the stage Bill Ryan and I held up today. In another decade there probably won't be any stages left.

The America we grew up in is disappearing, but I don't think I'll be alive to see it change much more. When I can't breathe or when I feel the pain building behind my eyes, I don't think I'll miss being alive, but I can't imagine a world without me, either.

I can't imagine going on without seeing you. Without riding beside you. You were there when I rode with Anderson and Quantrill. You were there at Northfield.

Ryan's a good man, even if he drinks too much, but it isn't the same without you.

Ryan and I stopped the stage between Mammoth Cave and Cave City when it rounded a bend. We leveled our pistols at the driver and the man riding shotgun. I told them, "Get rid of your weapons and climb down. We don't want to hurt anyone."

There were five passengers: a judge and his daughter, two other women and a salesman.

Ryan held his pistol in one hand and a pint of whiskey in the other. "Sure is good whiskey," he said, sipping at it while I collected the cash and valuables. "Would anyone like a drink?"

"This is an outrage," Judge Rountree said.

"I offer the man a drink and he calls it an outrage," Ryan said. "Sir, you have the manners of a Philistine."

"You'll see what kind of manners I have if you ever appear in my court," the judge said.

"I hope I never have the privilege of standing before you," Ryan said, "although I wouldn't mind seeing your lovely daughter again."

I said, "Judge, I'd appreciate it if you'd let me have that nice looking pocket watch."

"It was given to me by the governor of this state," he said.

"Well, then I'll be sure to treasure it. And, ma'am, that's a nice looking diamond. If you don't mind, it'd make a nice gift for my wife."

The lady gave me the ring but she said, "I can't imagine someone marrying a man like you."

"It's a mystery to me too, but I certainly thank you," I said and I bowed.

Ryan had taken another couple of drinks and he was getting boisterous. "Damn it, one of you people should have a drink with me. It isn't right for a man to drink alone. It's a bad habit. The next thing you know, I'll be drinking in the morning. You," Ryan said, pointing at the driver, "you look like a drinking man."

"I'm not supposed to drink on the job," the driver said.

"I'll tell you what. I won't tell if you won't."

The driver looked at the judge as if he were waiting for him to sentence someone.

"This is a drink that's going to be good for your health," Ryan said. "It's going to save you from a trip to the doctor's, if you get my meaning."

"Yes, sir." The driver took a long drink, wiped the mouth of the bottle with his hand, then took another drink.

"I didn't tell you to finish the goddamn bottle," Ryan said, taking it back.

I mounted my horse and said, "I want you to know we appreciate your graciousness. It's always a pleasure to meet people who know how to give."

After we rode off, Ryan and I counted the money and we had $803, plus the valuables we divided.

I told him, "It's good riding with you, Bill," but I felt empty. In the old days I was exhilarated after a good job, but the excitement's gone. Now the only thing that's left is the danger. I used to think it was better to be a hunted animal than a caged beast. I used to think most men spent their lives playing things so safe they put themselves in cages. They use their jobs and their families as an excuse not to be alive. But now they seem more alive than I do.

I'm not sure why I pulled my pistol on you, but I've thought about it a lot. I think it was because you seemed so contented. You knew what you wanted, even if it didn't make any sense to me, and you pursued it. I envied you when you said: "I like farming. It's what I am: a farmer."

I want to be at the race track, not in the fields with a bunch of darkies cutting down trees for some company from dawn till dark, but you're happy and I'm not. Frank, I know you're not "your brother's keeper," but I want us to finish the way we started: together.

Jesse

Prairie Grove, Arkansas
September 5, 1880

Dear Zee,

Major Edwards thought it would be safe to meet here, "And I like the irony of it," he said. "The bloodiest battle I was ever in took place here. It was late fall, but the day wasn't too different from this. There was the same blue sky, the same chill in the air.

"General Shelby was almost captured by the Union forces during that battle, but your brother helped save his life. Did you know that?" he asked, but he was talking to himself. Much of what he said was a monologue, a reminiscence, and all I could do was put a hand on his shoulder, sometimes as an act of friendship, sometimes to steady him. "It all seems so long ago."

"It's another era, Major. We're all older. I never imagined I'd feel this tired at 33."

Every few feet, the Major would stop to take a drink because he was hung over and he said, "There's nothing like the hair of the dog that bit you. It brings you back... from Indian Territory." He staggered a little. "The same way it takes you there. It's funny." He was shaking so badly he had to hold the bottle with both hands. "You sure you don't want a drink? Hell, Jesse, it's your birthday." He didn't wait for me to answer. "I used to say I'd never take a drink before dusk."

"Things change."

Edwards was wearing a suit, but he hadn't shaved and

the stubble on his cheeks gave his face a gray look. Or maybe it was the heavy drinking.

"Major, can I do anything?"

"No. No, I'll be all right." He picked an ear of corn from the field we walked through, examining it a moment, then tossing it aside. "The summer after the battle, they claim the corn that came up was red because so much blood had seeped into the ground. Do you believe that?"

"I don't know what to believe most of the time."

"Yes... it all seemed so simple years ago." He took another drink and gestured toward a woods that was half-cleared of timber. There was a big pine at the edge of the woods and you could see its needles stirring in the wind. The grass beneath our feet was withered and there were some graves alongside the woods. When we got to them, the Major took another drink, reading the markers silently, then he said, "To this complexion must we come at last."

I'm not sure what he meant, but I knew it had something to do with dying. Something to do with what made him so sad.

The Major pulled the brim of his hat down, shading his eyes. You could see the deep creases beneath them, and he looked a lot older than 41. He looked tired.

"Our boys are scattered everywhere," he said. "You'll find their graves in the hollows and on the hills, by the gulf and on these prairies. A lot of them don't even have a monument. But they don't need any. They made their monuments while they lived."

"I'd like to believe that," I said.

"They left a record for daring courage that the world's never surpassed. And you and I were a part of it.... You and I, Jesse." He took another drink. His hands weren't shaking so badly now, and there was a new light in his eyes. But I knew it would go away once he had a few more drinks. I know he's killing himself, but what can I say?

"The marvel to me," the Major said, "is that I'm not sleeping in a place like this. What have I been spared for when so many of my comrades were taken?"

"A lot of us ask that," I said, "but Cole says it's pointless. We were spared because we were spared."

"We'd find bodies with no wounds on them until they were turned over. Then you'd discover a single little hole behind an ear, a hole that brought death.... 'Two men shall be working in a field, one shall be taken and the other left.' That's Scripture. But it's also life."

He wiped tears from his eyes with a pale, shaking hand, clutching his bottle with the other. He said, "I think the most terrible death I ever saw took place here. One of our men (he couldn't have been more than 17) grew up a few yards from here and we could see his home and his mother standing at the window, watching the battle and waiting. He fought bravely, looking toward the window where he knew his mother watched. He'd been gone a long time. Almost within a stone's throw of his mother's door, within sight of the yard where he'd played as a boy, he was shot down... and he died.

"Are you sure you won't have a drink?" the Major asked again.

"What the hell, it's only once a year," I said.

He smiled for the first time, taking another long drink, then he handed me the bottle there next to all the graves.

"Happy birthday," he said.

Love,
Jesse

Nashville
December 1880

Dear Susan,

I went into Ray & Sons to buy some red oats when I saw Frank talking to Ike Ray in the office. I walked out onto the porch, rubbing my hands together to keep them warm while I waited for Frank. It was late afternoon and the sun seemed to be balanced on the horizon, like a silver dollar teetering on the edge of a table. You wait for it to fall.

Frank started to walk by when he came out of the grain store. He would have passed me if I hadn't put out my hand and said hello. He looked around to see if anyone was near us, then he said, "Jesse," speaking softly. "It's been awhile."

"I want to get it out of the way, Frank. It's always been hard for me to admit I'm wrong, but I want you to know... I'm sorry. For pulling my pistol on you."

"I forgot about it a long time ago."

He put an arm on my shoulder and we started walking down the street. Together. Generally, I don't like it when anyone touches me except you or Zee, but Frank's hand felt like it belonged there. "I got your letter from Kentucky," he said.

"Yeah. It was funny. I used to be happy anytime we were on a job because I didn't have the time to think about things. To brood. But it's different now. Even when Ryan and I were robbing the stage, I felt... sad. I wondered why I was there, I guess. It's a hell of a way to earn a living, but they won't let me do anything else."

"Sure, they will."

"No, you're just pretending. You'll see. We'll be riding together again and you won't even have a choice. It'll just happen. Someone will recognize you and you'll have to run. I don't know. A friend will betray you for the money. Some-thing will go wrong."

"You claim we can't quit and I think we have to. We've pushed our luck for years. If we keep at it, we'll be killed. It's that simple. For a long time I used to tell myself we were still fighting the war, like General Shelby when he refused to surrender and rode off to fight with Maximilian in Mexico. He picked the losing side there, too. The only war we're fighting is with ourselves, Jess."

"I always loved your optimism," I said.

When we got to our horses, we shook hands in the twi-light. Then we swung into our saddles, nodding at each other and I said, "I'll see you soon."

"I hope so. I genuinely do."

That night I lit some candles and fired at them behind the house. I wanted to see if I could extinguish the flame without knocking the candles over, but I'd only fired a few times when Zee came out.

"You'll scare the children," she said.

"A lot of men fire guns."

"Not behind their homes in the evening."

"Zee, the kids will be all right."

"Little Jesse began crying the last time—"

"THEY'LL BE ALL RIGHT, ZEE."

"Then stop for me. What about me?"

"I'll be in before long," I said. "Just give me a few more minutes. I want to get off a few shots."

She didn't answer me, going back into the house. After all these years, she still doesn't like guns. They make her nervous, and she keeps telling me I should sell some. But I need to be fast—and accurate. They're tools to me; I need them. The same way a carpenter couldn't get along without a hammer. Or a saw. I need my revolvers. And a shotgun. And a rifle.

I lit twelve candles, then paced off twenty feet. I watched the flame waver, sighted on it, fired. Sighted on the next one. Fired again. Then I listened. I couldn't hear the kids crying. After the screen door slammed, I didn't hear anything but my breathing. And the hammer cocking. And the shell exploding.

When both pistols were empty, I'd extinguished all the flames without knocking over any of the candles. "You haven't lost it yet," I told myself.

It reminded me of the time I was visiting Belle in Texas. She and Cole and the rest of the folks had gone to bed and I was left to snuff out the candles on the Christmas tree. Sixteen years later, things end the same way. I'm still standing alone in the darkness.

Jesse

Kansas City
April 10, 1881

Dear Susan,

Bill Ryan was arrested two weeks ago in a bar in White Creek. He ordered a dozen oysters and chased each one he ate with a glass of whiskey. The more he drank, the more belligerent he got, and Squire Erthman, who lived three miles down the road from Frank, arrested Ryan for disorderly conduct. When he was jailed, he had more money than "a man of his means" ought to and they discovered he was wanted in Missouri.

As soon as I heard about Ryan's arrest I told Frank, "We've got to leave here."

"It'll break Annie's heart," he said.

"It won't do Zee much good, either."

"We were beginning to feel we belonged."

"I don't think we'll ever belong anywhere again," I said.

"And you think I'm a morbid bastard."

"Yeah, well...." I shrugged.

"I told you they called Ryan Whiskeyhead for a reason. Told you you shouldn't have anything to do with him," Frank said.

"It doesn't matter who said what to whom... now. Does it?"

"I guess not."

"If you'd been with me instead of Ryan, this wouldn't have happened."

"Don't make it my fault. I didn't hold up that stage. And I sure didn't ask Whiskeyhead to be my partner."

"When I was a kid you always said I acted first and thought later."

"If you thought at all."

"Nothing has changed at least."

"Yeah, something has."

"What's that?"

"We've got to get out of here—fast."

Frank headed for Kentucky and I came here because... I don't know why. I told Zee, "They'll never look for me in my backyard," but she says I just wanted to come home, no matter what happens. I wanted to come home.

Jesse

Kansas City
July 16, 1881

Dear Belle,

I could almost hear the minutes of my life ticking away, even when I was a child; I had a strong sense of mortality but, since Northfield, minutes have become seconds, and I'm a man waiting. Sometimes I'm not sure for what. But there are a few things I still want to do.

I told Frank, "Every man ought to have a chance to fulfill certain promises, and there're a few I still want to keep."

"What're you getting at?" he asked.

"Let's take a ride on the Rock Island Line." We boarded the train at Cameron, a few miles from Winston. I'd heard the conductor on the train was William Westfall, who'd been a member of the crew that brought the Pinkertons to Clay County the night they threw a bomb into Ma's house and killed little Archie. I told Frank, "Maybe we'll get to fulfill a vow of ours tonight."

It only took us three months to get Daniel Askew, but he was too stupid to run away. Westfall wasn't in Clay County for twenty-four hours, and we never met him. But we'd seen his photograph.

Frank said, "Maybe we won't recognize him. He might have changed a lot in six years."

"I'll never forget him."

"Which one of us will go after the money?"

"If Westfall's the conductor, let's not worry about the money. This job can be a labor of love."

Frank and I sat in the smoking car. Waiting. We tried to read, but neither of us could concentrate. Then Frank started to tell me about Robert Ingersoll, describing his political career and his belief in agnosticism, but I couldn't concentrate on that, either.

"Who'd want to be an agnostic?" I asked. "Life's sad enough without the thought that all of this has been for nothing. That it's suffering and death and good-bye to your loved ones." But all I could think about was little Archie. And Ma's hand being blown off. The murdering bastards.

When the conductor entered our car, he came down the aisle slowly, like someone at a wedding who wasn't sure he wanted to be there. He paused next to me and said, "Your ticket, sir."

"Good news," Frank said.

I pulled my pistol out, sticking it into Westfall's gut, and said, "Here's my ticket."

"You can't do this," he said.

"Sure, I can. Watch me." Then I asked, "You're William Westfall, aren't you?"

"Yes," he stammered. "Who are you?"

"I'm the brother of the little boy you helped murder six years ago."

"I've never killed a little boy."

"Tell that to someone else." I stuck my gun into his back and said, "Walk toward the end of the car."

"I never—"

"WALK."

Frank and I followed him. I was grinning and I almost marched down the aisle, swinging my arms like I was in a parade.

"Some days it's great to be alive," I told Frank. "I think this is one of them."

When Westfall opened the door at the end of the car I said, "In case you haven't figured it out, I'm Jesse James," then I waited a long second and blew him into eternity.

"I wonder if he was an agnostic," Frank said.

"Damned if I know."

As Westfall pitched forward, I shot him a second time, watching his body fall off the platform into the long darkness, then, as the engine slowed, Frank and I jumped off the train, running alongside it on the earth William Westfall will never feel beneath his feet again.

Jesse

Kansas City
July 18, 1881

Dear Ma,

I was at the train depot a few days ago when I noticed a conductor who was missing the tip of the third finger on his left hand, like me, but my left hand was in my pocket. I said, "You aren't Jesse James, are you?"

"If I were I wouldn't be standing here all day taking tickets for the railroad, I'd be holding it up," he said. "Why'd you wonder if I'm Jesse?"

"Because I heard he accidentally shot off the tip of his third finger when he was a kid during the war. He was so mad he said, 'That's the dod dingus pistol I ever saw,' and everyone called him Dingus after that... I notice you're missing the tip of your third finger."

"I lost mine in an accident, and no one has ever called me Dingus."

"Well, I sure would like to shake Mr. James' hand someday," I said.

"So would I."

"Yes, he's a great man," I said.

"If he hates my bosses, he must be a great man."

"Yeah, bigger than life," I replied, smiling. "Why don't we shake hands with each other since I'm missing the tip of my third finger—"

"Ain't it a small world?"

"—and we can both pretend we've shaken hands with

Jesse James. I know it sounds peculiar—"

"Mighty peculiar, but I don't guess it'll hurt."

"It'll give us something to tell our kids."

"Mister, I think you might be crazy."

"You aren't the first one to say that," I told him, pumping his hand, then I got onto the train without turning around. I didn't want him to see how hard I was laughing.

Jesse

Kansas City
July 24, 1881

Dear Frank,

It's been almost two years since I met Billy the Kid, and I haven't thought about him in all that time.

Now I hear he's dead, shot by someone who'd been a friend. Even though I didn't like the Kid, he deserved better than that. I think he had a raw kind of courage, but it was as if he was always angry and didn't know who to blame for the circumstances of his life.

Friends had told him, repeatedly, to leave New Mexico the last year he was alive, but he wouldn't go. He just rode his horse around and around the territory in huge circles as if he didn't know what else to do. They told him he was going to die but he just shook his head and smiled that funny smile of his and kept riding, always in circles, as if he were trying to come back to some point where he could meet the self he'd lost.

"Don't we all die?" he'd asked.

It reminds me of something you quoted from Shakespeare once: "Take him for all and all, he was a man. We shall not look upon his like again." I can't say it any better than that. It doesn't matter if the Kid and I got along or not.

From what I've heard he was unarmed. I can imagine him wandering around Pete Maxwell's place in Fort Sumner on a night that was so hot he wasn't wearing any clothes.

Maybe he was moving from the bed of one senorita to another or maybe he'd gone out into the kitchen to get something to eat, the way some people have said, but I can see him in the moonlight. I can hear his high-pitched voice as Garrett approached him.

Billy said, "Who's there?" in Spanish, then Garrett pulled the trigger. Apparently, the Kid was dead the moment the bullet hit him. Blood spurted out of the neat little hole and ran down his stomach onto his penis, turning it red, someone said.

The Mexican women who were there got permission to carry his body across the yard to the carpenter shop, where they laid him out on a workbench and lit candles around his body, the flames pushing back the darkness for them but never again for Billy. Now it's eternal darkness because I can't imagine the Kid in heaven.

Garrett said, "You'd have thought that Billy was Jesus the way the women were all crying when I went to look at his body. Some of the women spit at me and swore although I told them, 'He was a dangerous man, a killer. I shot him mercifully through the heart, a clean shot. Look! I was just doing my job.' But they still spit at me and called me names."

It makes me wonder how much longer you and I will be able to hold out. Who will betray us? How will it happen? Will our wives (or someone else) be there to weep for us?

Lately, I've had the same dream over and over: The kids are running in and out so I take my pistol off because I don't want to frighten them. I go over to a wall to do something—I can't quite make out what it is—when someone across the room calls my name. When I turn around, all I see is a blinding flash of light.

Jesse

Kansas City
September 9, 1881

Dear Belle,

There were five of us: Frank and myself, the Ford boys and Dick Liddil.

We piled rocks and logs onto the track near Blue Cut two nights ago, then we placed warning flags in front so the engineer would slow down.

When the train stopped, Frank and Dick got the money from the safe in the express car and I went through the passenger car with Bob Ford, while his brother stood guard along the tracks. Neither of the brothers had been on a job with us before so they were excited. I could see Bob sweating and Charley kept firing his rifle into the air.

Each time Bob came to one of the passengers he'd say, "Hand over all your money or you'll die." He had a Colt Peacemaker with a seven and a half inch barrel and it looked big, awkward, in his hand. He might as well have been waving a cannon in the passengers' faces.

"You don't have to be so melodramatic," I told him.

"I thought that's how you did it," he said. "That's what all those books I read claim."

"Don't believe everything you read."

He looked more silly than menacing, but he's just a kid. I think the most exciting thing he'd ever done was squeeze his pimples and watch them break.

"I want to do everything right," he said. "I appreciate it when you let me know what I'm doing wrong," but I could tell he didn't mean it. I don't think anyone likes to be corrected.

"You're doing fine," I told him and hoped he wouldn't shoot his toe off.

One old fellow I came to was wearing a Confederate uniform and as he handed me his valuables I said, "I take it you were in the war."

"I had the honor of fighting with General Shelby, sir."

"You keep your money, then. I saw a lot of action

150

myself... at Centralia... and elsewhere. We never rob Southerners."

After we'd gone through the coach, I went up to talk with the engineer.

I handed him two silver dollars and said, "You drink to the health of Jesse James tomorrow morning." Sometimes I'm surprised by my audacity. (Or is it a kind of madness?) I said, "The boys and I will be glad to help your crew remove the rocks and logs from the tracks." I always say it never hurts to be magnanimous, especially since Bob and Charley could do all the lifting since they're so anxious to be part of the gang.

"I'd rather see you and your boys ride off," he said. "No offense, but you make a lot of the folks aboard nervous."

"All right, pard. Good night."

I jumped down from the engine, joining the others in the woods along the tracks.

When we'd mounted up I asked Frank, "Do you know what day it is?"

"Wednesday, isn't it?"

"What day of the month?"

He'd been quoting Shakespeare and when he does that, he never knows what's happening around him. Sometimes I think what happened to Macbeth or Lear or Hamlet is more real to Frank than what happens here. Sometimes I think it's a miracle Frank doesn't put his pants on backwards. Earlier, he'd been gibbering on about honor. He'd said, "What is honor? A word. What is in that word honor? Air. Who hath it? He that died o' Wednesday." It sounded as if he was mocking honor, but I don't think I've ever met a more honorable man than Frank.

"The day of the month," I said again.

Then he knew what I was talking about. "We were at Northfield five years ago today."

"Yeah." I smiled. "You can't say we're not improving with age. Yes, sir, just like fine wine."

"I guess we are at that," Frank said. I was almost sure

he'd have a quote for the occasion but, for once, he was speechless.

Jesse

White Cloud, Nebraska
September 25, 1881

Dear Belle,

"I like the look of that bank in Forest City," I told Bob. "We could take it."

"I thought you gave up on banks... after Northfield."

"You know what they say: If at first you don't succeed, try, try again."

"Then, if it doesn't work, you might as well give up. No point in being a damn fool about it."

"I don't think that's funny."

"Jesse, you know I'd go with you anywhere, but shouldn't you stick to trains? We're doing all right."

"It's a matter of honor. I need to take one more bank, and the one in Forest City doesn't have a time lock on the safe. It's almost antiquated."

Bob and I had looked at a lot of towns: Hiawatha, Pawnee City, this one. He'd wanted to take the train because it was faster, more comfortable, but I guess I'm old fashioned. And we were able to stop at small towns the train would have sped through.

I still like camping out when the weather's good because I can smell the air but Bob says, "You've smelled the air one place, you've smelled it everywhere. Give me a good hotel with a fine restaurant and a bar so I can have a couple of drinks after dinner. I can breathe in the air of some good cigars. Now that's something to talk about."

It's a new breed, Belle. Pretty soon they'll have to stick us in a museum along with the dinosaurs and dodo birds.

I told Bob, "I hear they're exhibiting a mermaid at Taylor Hall in Trenton, New Jersey. Wouldn't that be a wonderment?"

"Nah. Isn't a mermaid a woman with big tits and, from the waist down, she's got the body of a fish?"

I nodded.

"How would you get it in?" he asked.

"I never thought about that. I don't want to make love to her, I just want to see her."

"Hell, Jesse, you have to be more practical."

"Yeah, I guess so," I said. I wanted to tell him what it was like when I'd go off by myself sometimes when I was younger. I'd go up into the hills with a few provisions and some beer and just sit there. In the evenings I'd build a fire and the wood would pop. Sparks would explode in the air like fireflies. Once I spent a week in the Great Smoky Mountains on a high lonesome and I came back... different somehow. But I couldn't have explained it to Bob. I don't think he ever spent a day alone.

"You know, I'd like to buy a farm near here. Settle down."

"I thought you already tried that. In Tennessee."

"I did, but I've *got* to make it this time... for Zee."

"There're all these women in the world—some with big breasts, some with great legs, some with a great ass—and you're always talking about Zee. I don't understand you."

"I'm sure you don't."

I doubt that Bob has ever wondered about anything. If you asked him why we don't fall off the earth since it's spinning around, he'd look at you and say, "You must be crazy. What kind of a question is that?"

I remember Frank asked if I thought there was providence in the fall of a sparrow when he was reading *Hamlet*, and I thought about that for a long time. Bob wouldn't think about it at all. He'd say, "Who cares about a damn sparrow? I shot a lot of them when I was a kid."

Fuck it or kill it—that's Bob's answer for everything.

Jesse

Kansas City
October 15, 1881

Dear Frank,

We moved into our new house at night so none of the neighbors could get a good look at us. Probably you were wise to leave the state, but a part of me always seems to be missing when I'm not in Missouri. I ache for home (it's like having a bad wound) when I'm not here.

I guess we won't be riding together again. I know that, intellectually, but I refuse to accept it. I've spent my life refusing to accept what seem to me to be indignities but what other men, seemingly, suffer in silence. I don't know if I'm braver than they are—or if I'm a coward. But I can't live the way most people do.

I tell myself the new gang will work out, that Bob and Charley Ford will be all right. But I know I wouldn't have let Bob hold the horses a few years ago. It's not just his age, it's... a feeling. Now he's living with Zee and me.

Zee says, "I don't trust him."

"He's just young," I tell her.

It's early morning and we're lying in bed with the patchwork quilt pulled up beneath our chins. I'm thinking about getting up but I know the floor will be cold and I'll have to start a fire and... some mornings there doesn't seem to be any real reason for me to get up. To go on. But I know I will. The little things—pumping water, building a fire, reading the papers—help to sustain me.

"You were young when I met you," Zee says, "but you weren't like... *that*."

"Bob and Charley did all right at Blue Cut last month."

"Jesse, you're going to be sorry. There's something wrong with that boy. He's too... anxious."

"He just admires me."

"Maybe so. But there's something else. It's the way he looks at you, especially if he thinks you're not watching him."

"He just wants to be like me. He's even started to walk

the way I do, favoring one leg a little."

A horse neighs and I stiffen, reaching for my pistol beside the bed. I hold my hand there for a long minute, then I almost relax again. It's been years since I've relaxed completely. I don't remember what it's like.

Zee says, "Bob can look you in the eye without blinking. He can hold your gaze... for a long time... without looking away."

"That shows he's got an innocent heart."

"He never wavers, Jesse. It isn't right."

"Bob's a good boy." Am I trying to convince Zee? Or myself?

"It takes practice to do that," Zee says.

"It takes practice to do most things."

"I just wish he wasn't living here with us."

"If you're right and there's something funny about him, it's better he's here where I can keep an eye on him."

"You have to sleep sometimes. You can't always watch him."

"For God's sake, Zee, I've known him for more than two years. Each night, when we get the evening paper, we'll stop at the Topeka Exchange for a beer. He'll have two or three while I nurse one. I must have had a beer a day for the last month. I told Bob he's turning me into a drunk... A man lets his guard down when he's drinking. I'd know if something was wrong."

"You want to believe in him because there's no one else left now."

I get out of bed, putting my pants and shirt on, then I bend over Zee, kissing her. My bare feet are cold on the floor and I begin to shiver. Is it just from the cold?

I say, "I'll get the fire going and make some coffee... and say good morning to the dangerous Mr. Ford."

"You shouldn't joke about him."

"There isn't much to joke about these days, so I might as well joke about Bob."

"Joke about this," Zee says, hitting me with a pillow.

A few feathers float out from it.

I fall onto the bed, trying to grab her hands but she hits me with the pillow again and some more feathers fly around us. It's raining feathers and they're shining in the morning sunlight.

Now I've got Zee by the shoulders and she's squirming and the bed's shaking. I say, "We're going to wake the kids up," and she says, "I don't want to think about the kids."

We're laughing and it's almost the way it was fifteen years ago; for a moment, we can forget about the war and the rewards on my head and the lonesomeness. The old fears are gone, at least for a little while.

Now we're easy with each other. And with ourselves. I think: This is the way each day should begin. Without explanation. Without apology. Touching. New.

Jesse

Kansas City
October 28, 1881

Dear Susan,

I think things are closing in on me.

When Billy the Kid was killed three months ago, a lot of people said the west was coming to an end. Maybe it's true.

Two days ago there was a gunfight in Tombstone, Arizona. It only lasted about thirty seconds but when it was over three men were dead and another two were badly wounded. The papers say this might be the last great gunfight.

Wyatt Earp and two of his brothers, along with a dentist named Holliday, shot it out with the Clanton-McLaury faction at the O.K. Corral. The Earps and Holliday won, but some people claim they opened fire without giving the others a chance, but they have their defenders, too.

"Sometimes you can't tell the good guys from the bad,"

I told Bob.

"Yeah, look what they say about you. Some claim you're Robin Hood and others say... some pretty bad things."

We'd gone into the Topeka Exchange on our way home from getting the papers. I sipped my beer, then leaned my elbows against the mahogany bar, bracing one foot on the railing that ran along it.

Sometimes my whole body will begin to tremble for no reason if I don't lean against something. It's the way I felt when I had those high fevers and got the chills after I was ambushed at Lexington. Even my teeth will begin to chatter and, if I try to talk, I almost spit out my words. But this time I felt the seizure pass.

"A lot of people pretend to be what they aren't," I told Bob. I was still thinking about what had happened at Tombstone.

"What do you mean?" he asked. I thought he looked startled, but it's hard to tell with Bob. A lot of the time, I get the impression he's someplace else.

"I always hear you talking about what a great lady's man you are, but I never see you with any women."

He looked across the bar, finishing his beer. The foam on his lip made him look like he had a light mustache. I don't think he shaves more than once a week. He said, "You wouldn't expect me to bring them to your place, would you?" but I don't think he expected an answer.

It may sound strange, but I'm always reminded of being in church when I go into the Topeka Exchange. Maybe it's the soft light or the lustrous look of the wood. I almost understand why some men spend such a big part of their lives in bars.

I held up my glass and said, "When you look at the world through beer, it seems a lot softer."

"Or pissed on," Bob said.

"I love your romantic view of life. No wonder I let you follow me around."

Someone told me, "When you have a drink with a man, you're letting your guard down. You're saying you can trust the person."

I don't trust anyone, particularly with a five thousand dollar reward on my head.

"Doesn't it make you nervous?" Bob asked.

"If someone could betray Jesus for thirty pieces of silver, it isn't hard to imagine someone betraying me for five thousand, not even with eighteen hundred years of inflation."

"Yeah, a dollar doesn't go as far as it used to."

"Neither does friendship," I said.

Love,
Jesse

St. Joseph, Missouri
Christmas Day 1881

Dear Susan,

It's snowing.

Several inches have accumulated and Jesse Jr. and Mary are outside making a snowman. He has eyes made out of lumps of coal and a carrot for a nose.

I tried to get Bob to come out with us but he looked at the snow and said, "It's just a bunch of white crap you have to shovel. I don't see why people get so excited about it. A cousin of mine fell down and broke his leg on the way to the outhouse and to make things even worse, while he was lying there, he crapped in his pants."

I couldn't help smiling. "It can be a cruel world, Bob."

Last night, I dressed up in a Santa Claus suit. The kids and Zee had just finished decorating the tree when I went into the front room. "Ho, ho, ho, what have we here?" I asked.

"Daddy, Daddy, you look funny," little Jesse cried.

"I told you it was a dumb idea," Bob said.

I just ignored him, though. We turned down the lanterns, the wicks almost smoking, then we lit the candles on

the tree, then we exchanged presents. Mary tried to eat the
paper her jacks were wrapped in but little Jesse took it away
from her and said, "No, you don't eat *that*." I could tell it
made him feel grown up.

I've been trying to remember what it was like when we
were kids. I know we weren't moving from place to place—
there was a sense of stability in our lives—and we weren't
friendless. Perhaps this life hasn't damaged Jesse or Mary
yet, but we can't keep moving the way we have been.

There's a farm for sale near Lincoln, Nebraska. If I can
raise the money, I'd like to buy it. Maybe we could finally
stop running. You and Allen have done it. And it looks like
Frank has. Why can't I?

Next year my son will be in the first grade, and I want
him to have a normal life. It's something I pray for.

After the presents were opened, we stood around the
tree. Even Bob did, although I had to nudge him. If they
ever make a play out of *A Christmas Carol*, they can get
Bob to play Scrooge.

Zee and I held hands and we began singing: "It came
upon a midnight clear, That glorious song of old." Our
voices rose and fell. Rose and fell. "From angels bending
near the earth, To touch their harps of gold."

Bob stood there, moving his lips a little, but I could tell
he wasn't singing.

At the end of the song there was something about peace
and good will but, no matter how hard I tried, I couldn't
remember the words.

Merry Christmas,
Jesse

St. Joseph
Monday, March 27, 1882

Dear Susan,

You know how Ma can be. She gets an idea in her head

and she won't let go of it. I was visiting her and the family
with Bob and Charley Ford last weekend when Ma pulled
me aside.

It was twilight and the sky looked like a bloody rose,
getting redder and redder. I thought it was going to burst
into flame, the clouds shriveling up like burning petals, but
the light just gradually faded, the way our lives do.

Ma said, "I don't like that boy."

"You just don't know Bob."

"I don't know any snakes, either, but I know enough
not to lie down next to one so it can bite me."

"You've never liked anyone I've known. Cole was too
bawdy. Zee wasn't good enough."

"Trust your family," Ma continued. "That's all you can
trust."

"Zee *was* family."

"Well, that just proves what I'm saying. Look at how
she's turned out. She's stood by you."

I paused, tired. The two of us sat on the rockers on the
front porch. Rocking together. It made a kind of music.
Lulling. I remembered the way I used to rock Mary's bassi-
net. Back and forth, back and forth. It's one normal thing
I've done.

"For what it's worth, Zee doesn't like Bob, either. But
she doesn't know why. I've asked her to be specific, to give
me even one reason, but she can't."

"Women *feel* things," Ma said. "They have intuition."

Ma and Zee believe in omens. They can see death in
the bottom of a tea cup. All I can see are some soggy leaves.

"Then why didn't you know the Pinkertons were going
to throw that bomb into our house?"

I could see the tears welling up in her eyes in the twilight, but she held them back. Back. She never could show
much emotion, at least to me. Sometimes I thought I was an
accident. That Frank was the one she really loved.

Ma said, "Don't you ever talk to me like that again.
Ever."

I stopped rocking and walked to the edge of the porch. It was almost dark now, but I could see the lantern burning in the barn. Charley and Bob were out there with the horses. They were always off someplace together.

"I didn't come here to argue, Ma. I just wanted to see you."

She came up behind me. I could hear the boards squeaking under her feet, but I didn't turn around. Then I felt her hand on my shoulder, and I remembered the way she'd knead my shoulders when she still had both hands, before the Pinkertons blew one of them off with their damn bomb.

"I just don't want them to get you," Ma said. "It seems like everyone I know is dyin' off."

"I'm not going to die... yet."

"I pray for you... nightly."

"I need all the help I can get," I told Ma, "divine or otherwise." I gave her a quick hug and said, "If I never see you here again, I'll see you in Heaven," then I walked toward the barn to saddle up. I must have crossed that yard thousands of times—crying, laughing, lonely, on the run—in the more than thirty years I've been alive.

When Bob, Charley and I rode off, the sky looked like a giant piece of wrinkled canvas. There weren't any stars and lightning cut the sky in two.

The rain hit hard by the time we were about thirty miles from St. Joseph and we tied our horses in front of a small church we came to. We went inside, shaking the water off our slickers, and Bob said, "I hate this goddamn rain."

"You shouldn't take the Lord's name in vain," I said.

"That sounds funny, coming from you."

"Why?" I went to the altar and lit some of the candles. Outside, the lightning flashed faster than you could blink. Thunder shook the church.

"Because of the men you've killed," Bob said.

"They all deserved it."

"I wonder if they looked at it like that? Or their families?"

"I don't care how they look at it." I lay down on one of the pews but felt funny about it, so I sat on the floor, leaning against the wall beneath a stained glass window. When the lightning flashed, the shadow of the Cross stretched out in front of me. I closed my eyes for what I thought was a few seconds but I must have fallen asleep because when I opened them again, it was morning and the rain had stopped.

I went outside, walking through the muddy little graveyard beside the church. One of the tombstones said GONE ON TO GREATNESS and I thought about little Archie, resting in the shade of the juniper tree in the Mt. Olivet Cemetery. His tombstone says KILLED BY A BOMB.

I wondered what my epitaph would be but I got depressed thinking about that so I went back into the church. Nudging Charley and Bob with the toe of my boot. I said, "We'd better get riding."

Jesse

St. Joseph
Sunday, April 2, 1882

Dear Frank,

The wind's blowing from the south-east and it's raining. I pay a lot of attention to the weather because I don't have much else to do.

The temperature is 44 degrees and the sun rose at 6:10. I've sat around here doing nothing for so long, I'm beginning to feel rusty.

The barometer reads 30-74.

Miss Sara Bernhardt is getting married in London tomorrow. I hate myself for doing nothing.

I read the papers or pretend to read the papers. I spend hours sitting and staring. I buy the morning and the evening news. It's all the same.

I keep telling myself to do something, even if it's

wrong. I've made mistakes before and survived them, although surviving doesn't seem as important as it used to. A man needs a reason to be alive.

Maybe my luck will change if I do one more job. Bob and I have been looking at a bank in Platte City. This Tuesday there's going to be a sensational murder trial going on there. Bob and I could be in and out of the bank in minutes and Charley could hold the horses and serve as our lookout. There must be a hundred thousand dollars just sitting there... waiting for us... and it would be a three way split.

Do something. Even if it's wrong.

We can't go on like this. Even the children are restless. They know something isn't right. Last night at dinner little Jesse asked Bob, "Why are you always here?"

Bob just looked at his plate, hard, and bunched up his napkin.

"I liked it better when you didn't eat with us all the time."

"Stop that," Zee said. "You apologize to your Uncle Bob."

"He isn't my uncle. He isn't. Why is he always here?" His voice broke and Mary began to cry and Zee said, "Why is it we can never have a peaceful meal anymore?" Then she took the kids to their room and I got up from the table, nodding at Bob.

"I don't seem to be very hungry," I said. I sat down with the paper in the next room but I didn't look at it.

Bob came to the door and said, "If you'd like me to leave—"

"No, it's all right."

"I think I'll go out for a beer. Do you want to join me?"

"You go ahead, Bob."

I don't know why we've had him live with us. I guess it gives me someone to talk to now that you're gone. I'm away from everyone I love—Ma, you, Susan—except Zee. Bob's like a dog. You could kick him and he'd wag his tail.

I get so lonely... Sometimes I'll just sit here, oiling my pistol and wiping it down. Counting the number of shells I have left. Sometimes I think that's about all I have left: bullets.

When I tucked my son into bed I told him, "You shouldn't have said that to Bob."

"I don't like him being here, Pa."

"He'll be going... soon. Try to be patient. To understand."

"I love you."

"I love you, too."

Then I hugged him and kissed Mary and turned the lantern down. I didn't turn it off because they're afraid of the dark now.

There's a fine mist out as I walk down the hill toward where the Pony Express used to be. It's been more than twenty years. They claim they could have galloped around the world twenty-four times in the year and a half they existed. And now the stables are boarded up and weeds are growing through the cracks in the cobblestones out front. I stand there, trying to bring it all back: the smell of the horses and the hay and the men sweating, but it's all gone. Gone.

The rain has almost stopped as I head back up the hill. The old pain is back in my chest and I know I'll have to take some morphine by the time I get home. And there's the pain behind my eyes. And the other pain.

I can almost hear my heart beating as I walk up the hill and I begin to sweat. By the time I reach our house I'm bathed in perspiration.

Zee says, "You shouldn't have gone out in the rain. You'll catch pneumonia."

I mix the morphine and water, shivering. *To everything there is a season, and a time to every purpose under the heaven. A time to be born, a time to die.* I take the morphine without answering Zee.

Finally I say, "We all have to die from something," then I sink into a chair, waiting for it to be light.

Jesse

April 7, 1882

"Judgment For Jesse," *St. Joseph Western News*, April 7, 1882

When we approached the door leading into the front room on Monday morning, our eyes beheld a man lying on the floor, cold in death with the blood still oozing from his wound. Walking into the room and around the dead man's body, we opened the door leading into a kitchen where we found a woman with two small children, a boy and a girl.

At first the woman refused to say anything about the shooting but after a time she said "the boys" who had killed her husband had been living with them for some time and their name was Ford. Charles, she said, was a nephew, but she had never seen the other, Robert, until he came to the house with her husband a few weeks ago. When asked what her husband's name was, she said it was Howard.

When we asked her when the shooting was done she said, "I had been in the kitchen and Charles had been helping me all morning. He entered the front room and about three minutes later I heard the report of a pistol. Upon opening the door I discovered my husband lying in his own blood.

"I ran to the front door as Charles was getting over the fence, but Robert was standing in the front yard with a pistol in his right hand."

At this juncture the Ford boys made their appearance and gave themselves up to the officers and told them the man they had killed was Jesse James and now they claimed the reward. They said, "We feel proud we killed a man who is known all over the world as the most notorious outlaw who ever lived."

After breakfast, Jesse and the Ford boys had gone into the living room. Jesse took off his pistols, stepping up on a chair to dust a picture. When he did, Bob drew his pistol, shooting Jesse in the back of the head from about four feet away.

The marshal then asked the woman calling herself Mrs.

Howard if what the Ford boys had said was true.

Screaming at the top of her lungs she called them cowards and asked, "Why did you kill the one who had always befriended you?"

The marshal said, "They claim they killed him to get the reward money," then he lead her from the room.

Holding her little children to her bosom she said, "I cannot shield them much longer. Even after the Fords shot my husband who has been trying to live a peaceful life, I tried to withhold his name. But it is true. My husband is Jesse James and a kinder hearted and truer man to his family never lived."

This confession from the wife of the most notorious outlaw who ever lived created a profound sensation in the room. The thought that Jesse James had lived for six months within our city and walked our streets daily caused one to shudder with fear.

When the wife made her confession, we begged her to tell us about Jesse, Frank and the Ford brothers and she said she would. "The deed is done. Why should I keep quiet any longer? Charlie and Robert Ford have been here with my husband and while I never trusted them, little did I think they would kill him."

Jesse's body was neatly clad in a business suit of cashmere, of a dark brown substance which fit him very neatly. He wore a shirt of spotless whiteness, with collar and cravat, and looked more the picture of a staid businessman than the outlaw that he was.

The most renowned robber of his age, Jesse quickly rose to eminence in his gallant and dangerous profession and his exploits excited the emulation of small boys. Jesse was cut off in the prime of his strength and beauty, not by the hands of the hangman but by the shot of a base assassin of whom the Governor of the State of Missouri was the accomplice.

Two days after Jesse was murdered, he was buried at the James farm in Kearney. The Reverend R. H. Jones of

Lathrop read from the Book of Job: "Man that is born of a woman is of few days, and full of trouble." And the Reverend J. M. Martin of Kearney read a text from Matthew: "Therefore be ye also ready; for in such an hour as ye think not, the Son of Man cometh."

Because Mrs. Samuel feared her son's grave would be desecrated by souvenir hunters, Jesse James was buried in an especially deep grave. As his casket was lowered into the ground, hundreds of mourners—relatives, friends, clergy and even officers of the law—united in paying extraordinary honors to Jesse's memory.

Go thou and do likewise.

About the Author

A native Californian, Arthur Winfield Knight (b. 1937) received his M.A. in creative writing from San Francisco State University in 1962. He served as professor of English at California State University of Pennsylvania from 1966 to 1993. After he retired from teaching, he returned to Petaluma, California, where he resides with his wife Kit.

Knight, who is best known for his scholarship on the Beats, particularly Jack Kerouac (*The Beat Vision*, Paragon, 1987, and *Kerouac and the Beats*, Paragon, 1988), was editor and publisher of *the unspeakable visions of the individual*, a "bookazine" of beat scholarship and literary arts, from 1971 to 1988.

Since childhood, Knight has been interested in the outlaws of the 19th century, and he justifies his western writings as "switching from literary outlaws to real outlaws." His stories include "Remembering the Dead" (*New Frontiers, Vol. 2*, Tor, 1990, eds. Pronzini & Greenberg), "Buffalo Horns" (*The Montanans*, Fawcett, 1991, eds. Pronzini & Greenberg), Standing Alone in the Darkness" (*Christmas Out West*, Doubleday, 1990, eds. Pronzini & Greenberg) and "The Death(s) of Billy the Kid" (*New Trails*, Doubleday, 1994, ed. John Jakes).

His most recent book is *Outlaws, Lawmen and Bad Women* (Potpourri, 1993), a collection of poetry. In addition, Knight reviews films for the *Anderson Valley Advertiser, Potpourri, Caprice, Mystery Scene* and *Batteries Not Included*.

Also Available from **BurnhillWolf**

Shared Solitude
ISBN 0-9645655-1-X $7.95

Shared Solitude

D. A. Blyler's work is a collection of poetry, photographs and a one-act play referred to by Julie Kate Howard of the *Charlotte Poetry Review* as "a collection for those who have loved what they could not hold or found themselves holding what they could not love." Written with "a painter's eye," the work makes an attractive partner to *Verdon Angster*. Reichert himself has referred to Blyler as one "who knows what true intimacy between woman and man can accomplish, how profoundly one living presence can reveal vast hidden currents of sensation in another." *Small Press Review* says, "While his thrust...is alienation and difficult romantic relationships, his wit gives the book depth." The poems are complemented with "photographs of shrouded nakedness, icons of loneliness and images of veiled eroticism" (*Poet Magazine*).

68 pages, $5^1/_2$ x $8^1/_2$ paper

Verdon Angster

Marcus Reichert, a North Carolina artist and filmmaker, has produced a first novel that raises important questions about not only the foundation of identity, but the very mechanisms we use to create our notions of "self." Written with extravagant attention to language that is reminiscent of Virginia Woolf and Lawrence Durrell and filled with vivid, almost cinemagraphic detail, *Verdon Angster* chronicles the integration and disintegration of the 16-year-old protagonist against the backdrop of World War II and Europe in flames. Says award-winning columnist Harley Dartt, "*Verdon Angster* takes the reader on a provocative and disturbing trip to a place where our concepts of time, ethics, identity and reality are fluid and mutable. It is not a journey for the squeamish, but anyone who wishes to explore what it means to be an individual must come along for the ride. It's breathtaking."

248 pages, $5^3/_8$ x $8^3/_8$ paper

Verdon Angster
ISBN 0-9645655-0-1 $12.95